ENGLISH IN TOURISM

Check In

Christopher St J Yates

CASSELL

CASSELL PUBLISHERS LIMITED
Villiers House, 41/47 Strand
LONDON WC2 5JE

First published 1991

British Library Cataloguing in Publication Data
Yates, C. St J. (Christopher St John)
    Check In: a course for hotel reception staff.—
    (English in tourism).
    1. English language. Usage
    I. Title   II. Series
    428

    ISBN 0–304–33004–3

The Publishers gratefully acknowledge permission to use illustrative material from Holiday Inns International.

Illustrations by Peter Bull and Pan Tek Arts
Printed and bound in Great Britain
by Page Bros, Norwich.

CONTENTS

INTRODUCTION FOR STUDENTS

Read this before you begin the book!

1 WHAT YOU NEED

Check In gives you the English you need to do your job.

To use *Check In* you need

- this book
- the cassettes
- a cassette recorder
- a dictionary

2 THE BOOK

In this book there is

- **The working material**
  This is what you learn from.

- **Keys and tapescripts**
  This is where you look for the right answers to the exercises. The tapescripts tell you what is on the cassettes.

- **A grammar**
  This explains what you are learning.

- **Notes for teachers**
  Do not use this.

3 HOW TO USE THE BOOK

There are two kinds of exercise. One with the cassettes and one without the cassettes. The exercises with the cassettes are marked:

- **Exercises without the cassettes**
  a Read the heading.
  b Read the instructions.
  c Look at the exercise.
  d If you understand, do the exercise.
  e If you do not understand, use your dictionary and the grammar. Ask a friend.
  f Look in the Key and check your answers.
  g Go on to the next exercise.

- **Exercises with the cassettes**
  - **a** Read the heading.
  - **b** Read the instructions.
  - **c** Look at the exercise.
  - **d** If you understand, turn on the cassette and do the exercise.
  - **e** If you do not understand, use a dictionary or ask a friend.
  - **f** If you do not understand the cassette look in the tapescript. Use your dictionary. Start the exercise again.
  - **g** Look in the Key and check your answers.

4   HOW TO WORK

Do not try to do too much at one time. Thirty minutes is a good time to spend each day.

If you do not understand an exercise, ask a friend to help you.

Learn the words you need.

Use what you learn in your work!

Enjoy the book!

INTRODUCTION FOR TEACHERS

1 THE STUDENTS

Check In teaches the basic language required by front office staff within the hotel and catering industry. It is a companion course to *May I Help You?*, which is for bar and restaurant staff.

The materials are based on the relevant parts of the ICC* specifications for the hotel/catering industry.

Check In and *May I Help You?* are designed as self-access materials, as many, if not most, employees within the hotel/catering industry are not able to attend regular classes due to the hours they have to work.

2 THE MATERIALS

The materials consist of

- this book
- two cassettes

Students who may miss some lessons due to their working hours should also have a dictionary.

3 COURSE STRUCTURE

The course consists of ten Units. Each Unit normally consists of between seven and nine pages, divided into three stages.

a Pen-to-paper
This stage introduces new language for the students to absorb and practise.
b Cassette work
This stage involves work with the cassettes and is where the new language is recycled, together with language from previous Units. The exercises consist of 'on-the-job' tasks, such as taking messages, noting bookings and giving information.
c Letters
This stage consists of work on routine letters.

For the benefit of self-access students, full keys to the exercises and tapescripts are provided after the working materials. There is also a simple grammar explaining the point of the various exercises.

4 ASSUMED KNOWLEDGE

The course assumes some previous contact with English, either at school or through the work place. While minimal knowledge is assumed, this is not an absolute beginners' course.

---

* ICC—International Certificate Conference, a group of countries who have agreed common specifications and examinations for those working in the hotel/catering industry.

5 LENGTH OF COURSE

This will depend substantially on the existing level of English of your class when starting the course. Depending on this, the course will provide a minimum of 30 lessons, rising to 60 for weaker classes.

6 USE OF THE MATERIALS

While this book is designed mainly as a self-access course, it can also be used successfully in a teacher-directed class with teachers extending and personalising the course content. With a little imagination, other lively and enjoyable sessions can be developed where students are encouraged to build on their experiences. The following are a few suggestions for achieving this.

Personalise

Students can be encouraged to use knowledge of their own work situation in extensions of the coursebook exercises; for example, in Exercise 1 of Unit 1 students can describe their own jobs and hotels to the class, as well as the procedures used in their work place for booking a room. Students can bring realia, such as registration cards and hotel floor plans from their own work places and use these in group question and answer sessions. Students can recount situations where they have been required to give advice or to deal with complaints.

Where students are not yet working in the industry, teachers could ask students to prepare for individual lessons by collecting relevant information from a nearby hotel.

Increase oral content

Instead of writing responses to exercises in the book, students could answer orally or teachers could devise their own oral exercises, reserving those in the book for consolidation and homework. Oral responses could be made in a full class situation with the teacher playing the guest or, if students are confident, with students working in pairs.

Supplement

The book material can be supplemented with local material such as menus and maps collected by teacher and students. Exercises can also be supplemented by teacher-devised questions and situations similar to those in the book.

Extend

Teachers can develop exercises that challenge the students to go beyond the scope of this book. For example, situations can be extended through role play, initially with the teacher playing guest and the class responding. Later, as they gain confidence, students can work in groups with some acting parts and others observing and commenting. Finally, students can work in pairs or small groups with all students participating actively.

Depending on the ability of the students, situations can be made more difficult than those presented in the book, requiring the students to make more complex replies. They can also be asked to take the activity one step further; for example, in Unit 1 Exercise 9 students could write a reply to the telex and in Unit 2 Exercise 10 they could write a complete reply to a letter that the teacher has created. Students could also be asked to take down messages from the tape without using the prompts in the book.

Practise pronunciation

Teachers can use the exercises in this book to provide formal pronunciation practice and can also use such things as menus and tariff cards for practice of individual words.

Provide pre-listening opportunities

Students can be prepared for the taped listening exercises by introducing them to any vocabulary which teachers have identified as likely to be unknown and by practising any difficult pronunciation. Teachers could also devise their own mini-situations, similar to the taped exercises, for acting out before the taped situation.

UNIT 1

1 What do they do?

Look at the pictures below. They show people who work in the Holiday Inn Hotel in Manchester, England.

1 Chef   **2** Waitress   **3** Receptionist   **4** Porter

5 Cashier   **6** Barman   **7** Maid   **8** Lift attendant

Say what jobs these people do, like this:

1 *He's a chef.*
2 *She's*
3
4
5
6
7
8

Now say what these people do. Use the table below to help you. The first one is done for you.

The chef		all over the hotel.	He carries the luggage.
The waitress		in the bar.	She cleans them.
The receptionist		in the bedrooms.	He takes guests to the right floor.
The porter	*works*	at the front desk	*He cooks the food:*
The cashier	works	in the lift.	She serves the meals.
The barman		*in the kitchen.*	She prepares the bills.
The maid		in the restaurant.	He serves the drinks.
The lift attendant			She welcomes the guests.

9 *The chef works in the kitchen. He cooks the food.*

10 _____

11 _____

12 _____

13 _____

14 _____

15 _____

16 _____

2 The Grand Hotel

Look at these signs in a guide.

🛗	Lift	🏊	Swimming pool
📺	Television in the rooms		Conference facilities
WC	Toilets in the rooms		Air conditioning
☎	Telephones in the rooms	🚿	Showers in the rooms
🎾	Tennis court	⫶Ol **	Restaurant with two stars
🚗	Garage parking		

Now look at this information about the Grand Hotel. Say what facilities the hotel has got. Also say what it hasn't got, like this:

It's got television in the rooms.
It hasn't got a tennis court.

Tel: (0327) 60503, Telex 288441, 200 Rooms, 🛗 📺 🚿 WC |♦| ☎ ⫶Ol ***

1 _____

2 _____

3 _____

4 _____

5 _____

6 _____

7 _____

8 _____

9 _____

10 _____

11 _____

3 *What do you say?*

Look at these pictures and read the sentences. Then match the picture with the correct sentence, like this:

1 __d_____   2 _____   3 _____

4 _____   5 _____   6 _____

a May (OR Can) I give you our brochure, sir?
b May (OR Can) I help you, madam?
c May (OR Can) I give you your mail, madam?
d May (OR Can) I take your coat, madam?
e May (OR Can) I carry your luggage, sir?
f May (OR Can) I get you a taxi, sir?

4 *Tell the guest the way*

Look at this map. You work in the hotel. Some guests want you to tell them the way. Tell them where to go, like this:

GUEST: Can you tell me where the bank is, please?

YOU: *Certainly, sir. Turn right out of the hotel. At the crossroads, go straight over and the bank is on your left.*

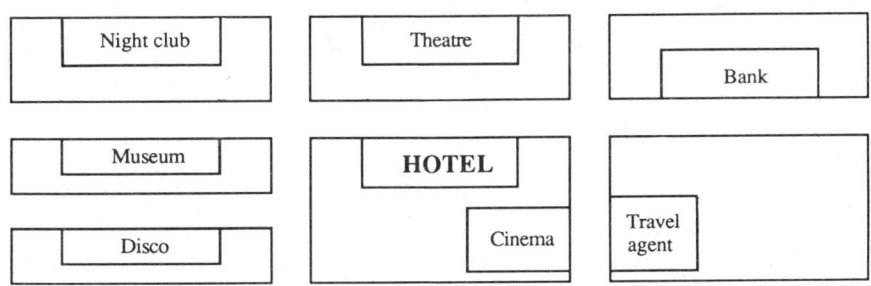

Now complete these sentences.

1 GUEST: Can you tell me the way to the cinema, please?

  YOU: Certainly, madam. Turn _____ the hotel. At the
  _____, _____ right and the _____ is _____ your right.

2 GUEST: Where's the disco? Can you tell me?

  YOU: _____. _____. _____
  the crossroads, _____ left. When you reach the junction, _____
  the road and the disco is _____ left.

3 GUEST: Can you tell me the way to the theatre?

  YOU: Certainly, sir. Turn left _____ the hotel. At the _____,
  turn _____. Go straight on and at the _____, turn right. The
  theatre is _____ your right.

4 GUEST: Where's the museum, do you know?

  YOU: _____, madam. _____.
  _____ the crossroads, go _____ on and the museum _____
  _____.

5 GUEST: Can you tell me how to find the travel agent?

  YOU: Certainly, madam, Turn right out of the hotel. At _____
  _____ _____ and _____.

6 GUEST: How can I find the night club? Can you help me?

  YOU: _____. _____.
  At the _____. Go _____ on and when
  you come to the _____, turn _____. It's _____
  _____.

5 What does the guest want?

Sally works at the reception desk in a hotel. A lot of guests ask her questions. Listen to the question on the cassette. Then read the answers below. Listen to the question again, and put a tick ☑ against the right answer.

1 The guest wants Sally to
  a tell him the way to the station. ☐
  b order a taxi for him. ☐
  c tell the taxi to take him to the station. ☐

2 The guest wants Sally to find out
  a Mr Smith's telephone number. ☐
  b Mr Smith's address. ☐
  c what number Mr Smith lives at. ☐

3 The guest wants
  a a double room for one night. ☐
  b two single rooms for three nights. ☐
  c a double room and two single rooms for three nights. ☐

4 The guest wants
  a a table for two for tonight. ☐
  b a table for two for tomorrow night. ☐
  c two tables for tomorrow night. ☐

5 The guest wants Sally to
  a give her a registration form. ☐
  b fill in her registration form. ☐
  c give her a pen. ☐

6 Take the message

Listen to these guests. They are asking you to take a message. Listen to what they say and write down the message.

1 Who is the message for? What is the caller's name and when is he arriving?
_____

2 What does the guest want you to do? When will he arrive?
_____

3 What is wrong in the guest's room? _____

4 Who do you send to the guest's room? _____

5 Where do you tell Mr Milewski to go? What is the guest's room number?
_____

6 When is the guest leaving the hotel? What does he want you to change?
_____

7 Conversations

Here are some conversations. Listen to the conversations and follow them in your book. Then rewind your cassette. Start the conversation again. This time, speak to the guest at the same time as the voice on the cassette.

RECEPTION: Good evening, madam. Can I help you?
GUEST: My name's Lawrence. I've got a reservation for a single room for three nights.
RECEPTION: One moment, madam. Ah yes, here we are. A single room with shower for three nights.
GUEST: That's right.
RECEPTION: Can you fill in this registration form, please, madam?
GUEST: Yes, right.

RECEPTION: Can you fill in the registration form, please, sir?
GUEST: Yes ... Oh, dear. It's all in German. Can you translate it for me?
RECEPTION: Certainly, sir. You put your surname here.

GUEST:	Right.
RECEPTION:	Your initials here.
GUEST:	OK.
RECEPTION:	And your passport number here. I can do the rest for you.
GUEST:	Thank you very much.

RECEPTION:	Can I help you, sir?
GUEST:	Yes, I've got a free day today. What sort of entertainment does this town offer? I mean has it got a theatre, for example?
RECEPTION:	Yes, it has. We've got an information brochure here, sir. It shows all the entertainment.
GUEST:	Ah, perhaps I can have a look at that.
RECEPTION:	Certainly, sir . . . Here it is. It's got information about the theatre, cinemas and of course excursions.
GUEST:	Ah, good.
RECEPTION:	We can get tickets for you, sir, if you like.
GUEST:	Good. I'll have a look and come back to you.
RECEPTION:	Thank you, sir.

8 A letter

First read this letter. Use your dictionary.

> 57 High Street,
> Culworth
> Daventry, NN11 6PP.
>
> 3rd March, 199_.
>
> Dear Sir/Madam,
> Please reserve one double room for myself and my wife, and two single rooms for my son and daughter, from 5th – 10th August, 199_.
> Please confirm my reservation.
> I look forward to hearing from you.
> Yours sincerely,
>
> *P.J. Knowles*
>
> P.J. Knowles

Now answer the letter.

Holiday Inn

CROWNE PLAZA®

Mr. P. J. Knowles,
57 High Street,
Culworth,
Daventry,
NN11 6PP.

5th March, 199-

Dear Mr. Knowles,

Thank you for your —————— of 3rd March.
I am pleased to ——————— your ——————— for two
——————— and one ——————— from 5th-10th
August, 199-.
We ———————welcoming you on 5th August.

Yours sincerely

---

9 *A telex*

First read this telex. Use your dictionary.

PLEASE RESERVE FIVE SINGLE ROOMS WITH BATH OR SHOWER FOR
THE NIGHTS OF 14 THROUGH 18 NOVEMBER IN NAMES OF HUCKER,
PHILLIPS, FORD, FOYLE, SIMPSON. THEY WILL ARRIVE ON
EVENING OF 14 BY FLIGHT BA 007.

PLEASE CONFIRM ABOVE RESERVATIONS SOONEST AND INFORM AS TO
WHAT CREDIT CARDS ARE ACCEPTABLE TO YOU.

REGARDS

WATSON

Now answer these questions. Put a tick ☑ in the right box.

I Watson wants you to reserve
  a five rooms. ☐
  b fourteen rooms. ☐
  c eighteen rooms. ☐
  d seven rooms. ☐

2 The guests will arrive on
   a 5th November. ☐
   b 14th November. ☐
   c 18th November. ☐
   d 7th November. ☐

3 The guests are coming by
   a car. ☐
   b rail. ☐
   c bus. ☐
   d air. ☐

4 Watson wants you to tell him
   a which credit cards the guests can use. ☐
   b how to reach the hotel. ☐
   c that the guests will all have showers. ☐
   d what facilities the hotel has. ☐

UNIT 2

1 What do you say?

Look at these pictures and read the sentences. Then match the picture with the correct sentence.

1 _____   2 _____   3 _____

4 _____   5 _____   6 _____

Speech bubbles: "...Mr Smith" / "...dinner start?" / "...about this city?"

  a At 7 p.m., madam. Would you like to reserve a table?
  b Would you like to give me your coat, madam?
  c Would you like to leave him a message, sir?
  d Would you like to follow me, madam?
  e Would you like to take this brochure, madam?
  f Would you like to fill in the registration form, sir?

2 Asking questions

Karen works at reception in the Holiday Inn, Frankfurt. She must often ask the guests questions. Complete her sentences below. Use the words in the box below.

> What   When   Where   How   Who

1 _____ would you like to pay, sir? By credit card?
2 _____ time would you like your morning call, madam?
3 _____ are you leaving the hotel, sir?
4 _____ are you meeting Mr Phillips, sir? In the bar?

5 _____ do you want the taxi to take you, sir? To the airport?

6 _____ is your room number, sir?

7 _____ are you expecting to meet you, sir?

8 _____ many guests are you expecting, madam?

9 _____ did you speak to about this, madam?

10 _____ did you make your reservation, sir? Last week?

3 Answering questions

Karen must also answer the guests' questions. Use the table below, and answer the guests' questions.

It We They	leave(s) close(s) cost(s) open(s) run(s) don't accept don't allow sell(s) take(s) don't charge	dogs, I'm afraid. personal cheques, I'm afraid. every half hour. at 5.30 in the afternoon. toilet articles in our shop. at 11.30 in the morning. from the main entrance. eighteen marks. most credit cards. for making travel arrangements.

1 Where does the airport bus go from?

_____

2 What time does the bar open?

_____

3 When does the bank close?

_____

4 Do you accept payment by credit card?

_____

5 Can I bring my dog with me?

_____

6 If I ask you to book me a ticket, how much will you add to my bill?

_____

7 How often do the buses go?

_____

8 Can I buy some razor blades?

_____

9 Can I pay by cheque?

_____

10 How much is breakfast?

_____

4 Answer the guests' questions

Read the guests' questions below. Then answer their questions. Use the words from the list below. Notice that the answers are in the past.

> close   reserve   take   ask   *arrive*   wait   order   go   book
>   want   clean   put   leave

1 Is Mr Smith here yet, do you know?

He _arrived_ ten minutes ago, sir.

2 Is Miss Olsen still here? I know I'm very late.

She _____ for half an hour, madam, and then _____.

3 Is the restaurant still open by any chance?

I'm afraid it _____ half an hour ago, sir.

4 Is Mr Seiko still waiting for me?

He _____ to the cafeteria, sir. He's waiting for you there.

5 What about the flowers I phoned about?

The maid _____ them to your room, madam.

6 Where's my taxi?

I _____ it five minutes ago, madam. It's coming now.

7 I think I forgot my briefcase. Have you got it?

Ah, yes, sir. I _____ it here under the counter.

8 Which room are we in?

We _____ a room looking over the lake, sir, as you _____.

9 Is my room ready yet?

Yes, sir. The maid _____ it early this morning.

10 How about my flight tickets?

We _____ you the flight you _____, madam. Here are the tickets.

5 Asking the guest questions

Read what these guests say. Then ask them a question, like this:

1 But I know I *reserved* a table.

What time *did you reserve* it for, madam?

2 But I'm sure I made a reservation.

When _____ it, sir?

3 I think I may have lost my handbag.

Where _____ it, madam?

4 I spoke to someone about this, yesterday.

Who _____ to, sir?

5 But I've already settled my bill.

I see, sir. How _____ it?

6 *Saying* no *politely*

Sometimes you must say *no* to a guest politely. Read what these guests say, and then answer, like this:

I But I wrote to you changing the date. Didn't you get my letter?

No, sir/madam, I'm sorry. I'm afraid we didn't get it.
_____

2 But I told my secretary to send you a telex. Didn't you receive it?
_____

3 Did you find my wallet last night?
_____

4 I know it was very short notice, but did you manage to book those theatre tickets for me?
_____

5 But didn't you know my wife was coming with me?
_____

7 *The registration card*

Karen works in the Holiday Inn, Frankfurt. Listen to her registering a British family. As you listen, fill in the registration card below.

✳ Holiday Inn®

REGISTRATION CARD

ROOM NUMBER	ARR DATE	DEP DATE	ADULT	CHILD	RATE	CODE Nº

PRINT BLOCK LETTERS ONLY PLEASE

SURNAME _____

FORENAME _____

PRIVATE ADDRESS _____

_____

```
COMPANY NAME & ADDRESS_____
_____
_____

OCCUPATION_____

NATIONALITY _____ PASSPORT № _____

CAR REG. № _____ NEXT DESTINATION _____
MY ACCOUNT WILL BE SETTLED BY
    [  ] CASH            [  ] CHEQUE *        [  ] COMPANY ACCOUNT *

    [  ] AMERICAN EXPRESS [  ] DINERS CLUB    [  ] VISA        [  ] ACCESS

    [  ] OTHER C/C                   * BY PRIOR ARRANGEMENT

SPECIMEN SIGNATURE                               CLERK'S INITIALS

MPL 94
```

8 *Take the message*

Listen to these guests and write down what they want you to do.

Holiday Inn

1 What is the guest's room number and what is wrong? _____

2 What is the guest's name? What kind of room does he want and when does he want it? _____

3 The message is for _____ in room _____ from Mr _____. He _____ because _____. He says he is very _____ and will _____.

4 Who is the message for? Where should the guest go and when should she arrive? _____

5 Who should Mr Marchant ring, in what country, and on what number? _____

6 What does the guest want and what is his room number? How much can you spend? _____

Here are some conversations. Listen to the conversations and follow them in your book. Then rewind your cassette. Start the conversation again. This time, speak to the guest at the same time as the voice on the cassette.

RECEPTION: Holiday Inn, can I help you?
GUEST: Good evening. I was wondering if you had a single room free for two nights.
RECEPTION: When did you want to come, sir?
GUEST: Tomorrow, actually.
RECEPTION: I'm very sorry, sir. We're fully booked at the moment. Can I suggest you try our other hotel in Frankfurt?
GUEST: Is it near the city centre?
RECEPTION: It's not far, sir. It's by the conference centre.
GUEST: That sounds OK. Can I have the number?
RECEPTION: Certainly, sir. It's Frankfurt, which is 69, and then 68 02 0.
GUEST: I'll give them a call. Thank you for your help.
RECEPTION: Not at all, sir. Goodbye.

GUEST: Excuse me, I'm supposed to be meeting a Mr Altmann here. Can you point him out to me?
RECEPTION: Certainly, sir. He's the tall, dark man wearing glasses, over there, carrying a briefcase.
GUEST: Er, ah, yes, I see him, thank you.
RECEPTION: It's no trouble, sir.

GUEST: Can you tell me where I can find Miss Grant, please?
RECEPTION: Miss Grant, madam? Yes, she's the small, blonde lady standing by the boutique.
GUEST: I don't see her.
RECEPTION: Over there, madam. She's wearing a red dress and carrying a mackintosh.
GUEST: Ah, yes, I've got her. Thanks.
RECEPTION: Not at all, madam.

GUEST: Morning. What time do you serve lunch?
RECEPTION: From 12 o'clock, madam. From 12 till 2 in both restaurants.
GUEST: There are two restaurants?
RECEPTION: Yes, madam. One here on the ground floor, and the other on the first floor.
GUEST: Ah, right. Thank you. What about room service?
RECEPTION: That's a 24-hour service, madam. Just ring from your room.
GUEST: I may do that. Thank you.
RECEPTION: Thank you, madam.

First read this letter. Use your dictionary.

MAIN-TAUNUS-ZENTRUM

Mrs P. R. Laporte,
12 Boulevard de la Republique,
83240 Cavalaire/s/mer,
France

Dear Mrs Laporte,

Thank you for your letter of 10th August.

I regret that we are fully booked for the period 10th–15th August, and are therefore unable to offer you accommodation.

May I suggest you try our other hotel in Frankfurt? The address is
Mailander Strasse 1,
6000 Frankfurt/Main 70
Telephone (069) 68 02 0

I am sorry we cannot help you at the moment, but hope you will stay with us the next time you come to Frankfurt.

Yours sincerely,

Now complete the following fax. Use words from the letter above.

SENT BY: XEROX Telecopier 3562;   21/06/91 ; 10:30 ; 0044   06196 72996

MAIN-TAUNUS-ZENTRUM

Dear Mr Svensson,

_____ you _____ your letter of 1st May. I _____
our accommodation is fully _____ for the _____ 1st–4th July.
I am afraid we cannot therefore _____ you in this instance.

May I _____ you _____ to _____ a reservation
in our other hotel in Frankfurt? I enclose our hotel directory showing the

_____ .

We _____ you will stay with us the next time you come to Frankfurt.

_____ ,

11 A telex

Now complete the following telex.

```
REGRET WE ARE ————————— TO ACCEPT YOUR —————————
FOR 15TH MARCH AS WE ARE ——————— .  I ———————
YOU TRY OUR ——————— HOTEL  IN  FRANKFURT,  TELEX
NUMBER 411805.


REGARDS
```

UNIT 3

1 Asking questions

Look at these pictures and read the sentences. Then match the pictures with the correct sentence.

a Have you lost your mother?
b Have you filled in the registration card, madam?
c Have you arranged to meet him here, sir?
d Have you left your briefcase, sir?
e Have you made a reservation, sir?
f Have you settled the bill, sir?

2 Some more questions

Sometimes you want to ask a guest a question. Write questions using *have* or *has*, like this:

Make a reservation?
Have you made a reservation, sir/madam?

1 Your guest arrive?

_____

2 Look in the bar?

_____

3 Order a taxi?

_____

4 Collect all your luggage?

_____

5 See our information booklet?

_____

6 Leave it in your room?

_____

3 What's the best answer?

Look at what these guests say to you. Then choose the best answer from the table below, like this:

Still no answer from Mr Kuypers?
I've tried his room several times, sir/madam.

_____

	given	it for 6.30, sir.
	told	a room overlooking the lake, madam.
I've	sent	them up to your room, sir.
	reserved	your flight to AF 345, sir.
	changed	the chef to prepare her meals specially, sir.
	ordered	her your message, madam.

1 I told you my wife needs special food, didn't I?

_____

2 I asked for a room with a view.

_____

3 Have you contacted Mrs Haynes?

_____

4 Any news of my tickets?

_____

5 Did you arrange a taxi for us?

_____

6 Did you get those flowers?

_____

4 Some short answers

Sometimes you don't need to answer your guest with a full sentence. Use short answers with these guests, like this:

Has my guest arrived?
No, sir/madam, I'm afraid he/she hasn't.

_____

1 Have you contacted Miss Roberts?

_____

2 Has the restaurant opened yet?

_____

3 Have my colleagues got here yet?

_____

4 Did you find my umbrella?

_____

5 Has my husband come yet?

_____

6 Has the fax I'm expecting come yet?

_____

5 *He may have gone to the bar*

Melina works in the front office of the Holiday Inn in Athens. Sometimes people ask her questions which she cannot answer. But she tries to be helpful, like this:

Where can I find Mr Georgiou?
go/bar
I don't know, sir/madam. He may/could have gone to the bar.

_____

Now you answer the questions.

1 Do you know where my wife is?
   go/restaurant

_____

2 Do you know where Mr Hussein is?
   leave/hotel

_____

3 Where's Miss Altobello?
   decide/go out

_____

4 I left my mackintosh here. Do you know where it's gone?
   my colleague/take/cloakroom

_____

5 Where can I find Mrs Macdonald?
   stay/room

_____

6 Why isn't Mr Kamori here?
   cancel/reservation

_____

6 Talking to guests

Complete the following sentences. Use these words:

> somewhere/something   someone/somebody   nothing   no one/nobody
> nowhere   anywhere   anyone   anything

1 Your handbag, madam? I'm sure _____ will find it soon.

2 I'm afraid we can't do _____ to help, sir.

3 Your wife, sir? I'm afraid _____ has seen her.

4 The flight is full, madam. I'm afraid there's _____ we can do.

5 We'll find him, sir. I'm sure he's _____ in the hotel.

6 I'm sorry, sir. There isn't _____ who wants to share a taxi.

7 I'm sure there's _____ we can arrange, madam.

8 I'm afraid Miss Lockhart is _____ in the hotel, sir.

9 I'm afraid there isn't _____ in the hotel large enough for a banquet, madam.

7 At the cashier's

Christine works as a cashier in the Holiday Inn, Paris. Listen to these guests asking her questions. Then read the answers in your book. Listen to the question again and put a tick ☑ against the right answer.

1 The guest wants to
  a change dollars into francs. ☐
  b change francs into dollars. ☐
  c change marks into francs. ☐

2 The guest wants to
  a change Japanese yen. ☐
  b buy Japanese yen. ☐
  c know what the exchange rate is. ☐

3 The guest's cheque is in
  a lire. ☐
  b dollars. ☐
  c pesetas. ☐

4 The guest wants to pay by
  a traveller's cheques. ☐
  b credit card. ☐
  c cash. ☐

5 The guest is saying his bill is wrong because
  a he hasn't visited the restaurant. ☐
  b he doesn't drink. ☐
  c he doesn't smoke. ☐

8 _Take the message_

 Listen to these guests and write down what they want you to do.

 Holiday Inn

1 The guest's flight has been _____. He wants you to _____
   _____. He will arrive _____.
2 Does the guest need: **a** dinner? ☐ **b** a waiter? ☐ **c** the maid? ☐
3 The guest is Mr _____ in room _____. Mr Ito will
   ring at _____. The guest wants you to: **a** tell Mr Ito to ring again
   at 7. ☐ **b** tell Mr Ito the guest will ring him at 7. ☐ **c** tell Mr Ito the guest will
   ring him tomorrow. ☐
4 The caller wants to hold a _____. She wants to know about your
   _____ and _____.

9 _Some conversations_

 Here is a conversation. Listen to the conversation and follow it in your book. Then
rewind your cassette. Start the conversation again. This time, speak to the guest at the
same time as the voice on the cassette.

GUEST: Good morning.
CASHIER: Good morning, sir. Can I help you?
GUEST: I hope so. Can you change these dollars into francs for me?
CASHIER: Certainly, sir.
GUEST: What's your exchange rate?
CASHIER: Today it's five francs eighty to the dollar.
GUEST: OK.
CASHIER: How much do you want to change, sir?
GUEST: A hundred dollars.
CASHIER: Right, sir. That's five hundred and eighty francs.
GUEST: OK.
CASHIER: Thank you, sir.

Now read these sentences. Then listen to this guest. Choose the sentence that best
answers what the guest says. Say that sentence onto the cassette. You will then hear
the right answer. Read the sentences now.

> How much is the cheque for, madam?
> That's right, madam. Here you are, and thank you.
> Good afternoon, madam. What can I do for you?
> It's ten francs to the pound.

21

Now look at the next group of sentences. Then listen to the next guest. Again, choose the sentence that best answers what the guest says. Say that sentence onto the cassette. You will then hear the right answer. Read the sentences now.

> One moment, sir. Here it is. How would you like to pay?
> That'll be fine, sir.
> Good morning, sir.
> Let me just check. Oh, I am sorry, sir. This receipt
>   has been put in the wrong place. It's for room double three two.
> Certainly, sir. What's your room number?
> Yes, of course, sir. One moment, please, and I'll change it.

10 A letter

First read this fax. Use your dictionary.

SENT BY: XEROX Telecopier 7017;   '90 08/13 10:54   0223 670768   ALPHA ENG

Alpha Engineering Ltd

PO Box 421, Oxford OX1 3BB, England.
Tel: (0865) 35627. Telex: 267358 ALPHENG

The Marketing Manager,
Holiday Inn Hotel,
10 Place de la Republique,
75541 Paris,
France

Dear Sirs,

We are looking for a suitable hotel for **our** 199– European sales conference, and would be grateful if you could send us details of your hotel, its conference facilities, and also details of entertainment facilities in Paris.

Yours faithfully,

M. Langhan

M. Langan (Miss)

Now answer the fax. Use these words:

excellent	facilities	enquiry	stay	service	size	rate	cost
have/has got	interest	hope	modern	comfortable		quote	group
		transport	hear				

VELIZY

Mrs M. Langan,
Alpha Engineering Ltd.,
PO Box 421,
Oxford OX1 3BB,
England.

Dear Miss Langan,

Thank you very much for your _____ of 16th February.

As you will see from the enclosed brochure, our hotel is a large,
_____ one right in the city centre. _____ to and from the
airport is easy, as we run our own free bus _____ every half
hour.

Our _____ for conferences are, we like to think, _____ .
We can accommodate _____ of 20 to 100, as we _____ four
conference rooms of different _____ in the hotel.

Each room _____ its own shower, television and minibar to make
our guests' _____ as _____ as possible.

For groups of more than 50, we are pleased to _____ a special
_____ . Perhaps you can let me know how many representatives
of your company there will be, so that I may send you details of
_____ .

I enclose details of Paris, which I _____ will be of
_____ to you. I look forward to _____ from you again.

Yours sincerely,

Michel Legrand
Marketing Manager

UNIT 4

1 What do you say?

Look at these pictures and read the sentences. Then match the pictures with the correct sentence.

1 _____	2 _____	3 _____
4 _____	5 _____	6 _____

a I'll post it for you, sir.
b I'll reserve one for you, sir.
c I'll send the maid, sir.

d I'll get you the bill, madam.
e I'll order one immediately, madam.
f I'll leave him a message, madam.

2 Saying what you will do

Look at what these guests say. Use the table below, and say what you will do to help them.

	give	some up immediately, madam.
	make	the travel agent for you, madam.
	take	his room for you, madam.
I'll	send	an appointment with the barber for you, sir.
	try	him to call you when he returns, sir.
	put	it to the cloakroom, sir.
	ring	them the message, madam.
	ask	you through to the restaurant, sir.

1 Can you put my coat somewhere?

2 There's no soap in my room.

_____

3 Is Mr Sanchez there?

_____

4 Do you have a table for six for tonight?

_____

5 Please tell my guests I'll wait for them in the bar.

_____

6 Please tell Mr Yamamoto to telephone me urgently.

_____

7 Can you change these tickets for me?

_____

8 Can I get a haircut in the hotel?

_____

3 Giving advice

Sometimes guests ask for advice. Look at what these guests say. Then give them advice, using the notes and one of the sentences, like this:

I Is there anything to see in this city?
visit/old city
It's worth visiting the old city, sir/madam. It's very lively.

_____

These are the sentences to use:

It's got some beautiful windows.	They're very cheap here.
They're very competitive.	There's an exhibition then.
There are some beautiful views.	Public transport is not
It's very lively.	very good in the country.

2 I'd like to get out of the city for a day. Where do you suggest I go?
go/mountains

_____

_____

3 How far in advance do I need to reserve a room in October?
book/as early as possible

_____

_____

4 How can I get into the country for a day?
hire/car

_____

_____

5 Are there any sights in the city?
visit/cathedral

_____

_____

6 How do I get from the airport to your hotel?
take/taxi

_____

_____

7 Your rates for conferences seem expensive to me.
compare/them

_____

_____

4 Asking what the guest prefers

Sometimes you need to ask guests what they prefer. You can do that like this:

I'd like a single room for the night, please.
Would you prefer/rather a room with a shower or a bath, sir?

Now ask what these guests would prefer. Use the table below.

Would you	prefer rather	the morning or the afternoon trip, sir? in the restaurant or outside, sir? one room or separate rooms, sir? the afternoon or the evening show, madam? to pay cash or by credit card, madam?

I Then we'll need somewhere for the two children.

_____

2 I'd like to settle the bill, please.

_____

3 I'd like to book a table for this evening, please.

_____

4 My wife and I would like to go on this trip to the mountains.

_____

5 We'd like to go to the theatre on Saturday.

_____

5 Offering to help

Look at these pictures and read the sentences. Then match the pictures with the correct sentence.

1 _____

2 _____

3 _____

4 _____

5 _____

6 _____

a Shall I give him a message?
b Shall I book your tickets for you?
c Shall I ring the railway station?
d Shall I fill it in for you?
e Shall I show you on the map?
f Shall I show you the way?

6 At reception

 Takako works in the Holiday Inn, Tokyo. Listen to these guests asking her questions. Then read the answers in your book. Listen to the question again and put a tick ☑ against the right answer.

1 The guest wants Takako to
  a confirm her flight for tomorrow. ☐
  b postpone her flight for three days. ☐
  c get her a seat on flight JL 511. ☐

2 The guest wants to go to Hong Kong
  a today. ☐
  b tomorrow. ☐
  c the day after tomorrow. ☐

3 The guest wants to go to Osaka
  a this morning. ☐
  b at 3 o'clock tomorrow afternoon. ☐
  c tomorrow morning. ☐

4 The guest wants to
   a do some sightseeing away from the city.   ☐
   b visit the countryside.   ☐
   c go on a trip round the city.   ☐

5 The guest wants Takako to
   a cancel his flight.   ☐
   b get him a seat on flight BA 007.   ☐
   c confirm his flight.   ☐

7 Take the message

 Listen to these guests and write down the message.

Holiday Inn

1 The guest wants you to _____ his seat on flight _____.

2 The guest wants you to reserve _____ places on trip _____.

3 The guest wants: **a** to postpone his flight. ☐ **b** to go to London as quickly as possible. ☐ **c** to confirm his flight. ☐

4 Write down the telex.

NUMBER: _____ ANSWERBACK: _____

ATTENTION: Mr _____

_____

_____

REGARDS

_____

8 Some conversations

 Here is a conversation. Listen to the conversation and follow it in your book. Then rewind your cassette. Start the conversation again. This time, speak to the guest at the same time as the voice on the cassette.

RECEPTION: Good evening, Holiday Inn.
GUEST: Evening. Do you have two double rooms free for tonight, by any chance?
RECEPTION: One moment, sir. I'll just check for you. . . . Hello, sir?
GUEST: Hello.
RECEPTION: I'm afraid we haven't got two double rooms, sir. We've got one double room and two singles, though.

GUEST:	Well, that'll do. Can I reserve them now?
RECEPTION:	Certainly, sir. Can I have your name?
GUEST:	Peters.
RECEPTION:	Mr Peters. Thank you, sir.
GUEST:	I'm leaving the station now and expect to arrive in about half an hour.
RECEPTION:	We'll expect you then, sir.

Now read these sentences. Then listen to this guest. Choose the sentence that best answers what the guest says. Say that sentence onto the cassette. You will then hear the right answer. Read the sentences now.

> Certainly, madam. Would you prefer a weekend excursion, or a one day trip?
> Of course, madam. Tell me what you'd like, and I'll make the booking.
> Good afternoon, madam. How can I help you?
> We've got a lot of one day excursions. I'll give you the brochure, and then you can choose the one you prefer.

Now look at the next group of sentences. Then listen to the next guest. Again, choose the sentence that best answers what the guest says. Say that sentence onto the cassette. You will then hear the right answer. Read the sentences now.

> The morning flight. I'll ring the airline, sir, and see what I can do.
> I can certainly try, sir. Would you prefer economy, business or first class?
> I'll ring you as soon as I know anything, sir.
> There's a morning and an evening flight, sir. Which would you prefer?

9 A letter

First read this letter. Use your dictionary.

Smith Plastics Inc.   2432 25th Avenue, Belmont 02178, Massachusetts, U.S.A.

The Marketing Manager,
Holiday Inn,
1–13–7 Hatchobori,
Chuo-ku,
Tokyo 104,
Japan.

Dear Mr Nashida,

Thank you for your letter of 20th February regarding our Tokyo Sales Conference in May. We are pleased to accept your offer.

In addition, we would like to hold a formal banquet on the last day of the conference. Perhaps you could let me have sample menus as soon as possible.

Yours sincerely,

A.J.Dutton

A. J. Dutton
Marketing Director

Now write a telex answering the letter. Use these words:

offer	pleased	of	menus	thanks	sample

MANY _____ FOR YOUR LETTER _____ 20TH
FEBRUARY. WE ARE VERY _____ THAT YOU HAVE
ACCEPTED OUR _____ . _____ _____
WILL BE SENT TO YOU IN THE NEXT FEW DAYS.

REGARDS

Now complete this letter. Use these words:

menus	tastes	further	see	included	may	welcome
enclose	food	pleased	cater			

Holiday Inn

YAESU

Dear Mr Dutton,

_____ to my telex, I _____ sample _____ as requested.

We would _____ any comments you may have on these, and would
be _____ to make any changes you _____ want.

You will _____ that we have _____ a mixture of Japanese and
Western _____ , our purpose being to _____ for different
_____ .

I look forward to hearing from you.

Yours sincerely,

Y. Nishida

_____
Y. Nishida,
Marketing Manager

UNIT 5

1 *Where is it located?*

Look at this plan of a hotel. Then say where the facilities are located, like this:

Where's the reception desk?
The reception desk is situated/located on the ground floor.

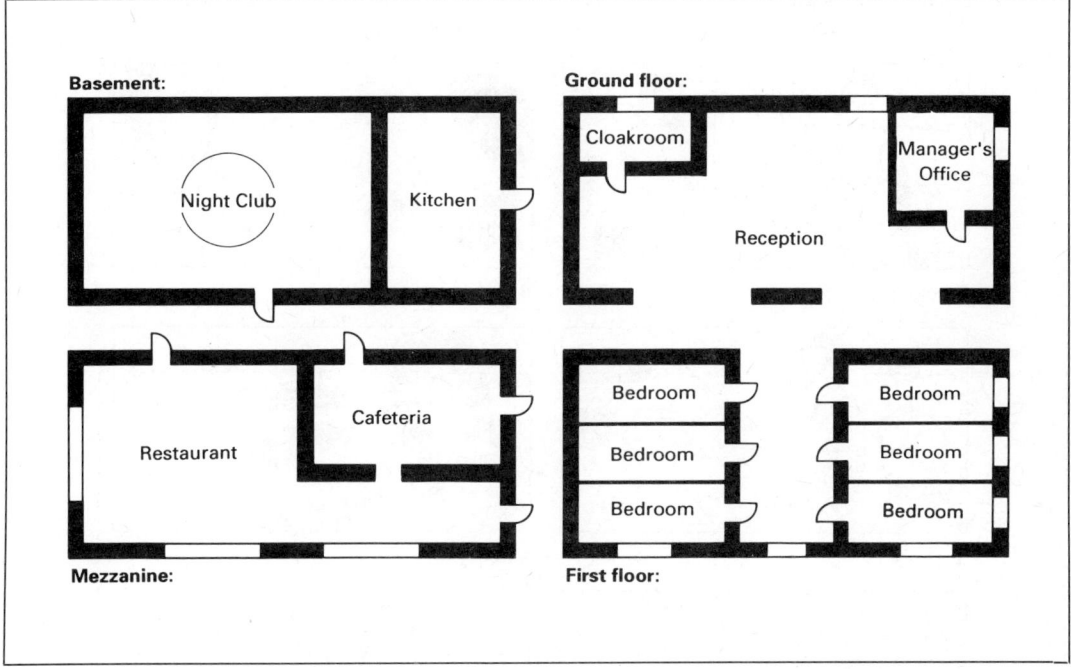

I Where's the kitchen?

_____

2 Where's the restaurant?

_____

3 Where's the manager's office?

_____

4 Where are the bedrooms?

_____

5 Where's the night club?

_____

6 Where's the cafeteria?

_____

7 Where's the cloakroom?

_____

Look at these pictures and the words below them. Then say what happens when guests arrive.

1 meet/entrance

2 show/reception

3 welcome/reception

4 give/registration card

5 check in

6 hand/key

7 take/lift

8 show/room

1 *They're/They are met at the entrance.*

2 _____

3 _____

4 _____

5 _____

6 _____

7 _____

8 _____

3 Giving advice

Sometimes guests ask for advice. Give these guests advice, like this:

I Where can I leave my coat?
leave/cloakroom
I should leave it in the cloakroom, sir/madam.

_____

2 Where can I get some local information?
ask/reception

_____

3 I've lost my cheque book.
enquire/lost property office

_____

4 What can I get to eat in my room?
ring/room service

_____

5 Is there a flight to Athens today?
call/airport

_____

6 Where can I find a Mr Li?
go/meeting point

_____

7 I want to discuss a wedding reception.
see/manager

_____

4 Where was it found?

Sometimes guests lose things. Ask these guests whether what you have found belongs to them, like this:

hat; leave/in the restaurant
Is this your hat, sir/madam? It was left in the restaurant.

_____

I documents; leave/in the bar

_____

2 suitcase; find/in the foyer

_____

3 keys; hand in/at reception

_____

4 jacket; discover/in the night club

_____

5 coats; put/in the cloakroom

_____

5 More advice

First read the sentences below. Then listen to these guests. Choose the sentence that best answers the guest. Say the sentence onto the cassette. You will then hear the right answer.

> I should speak to the manager, madam. Shall I put you through to him?
> I should contact the airline, sir. Shall I call them for you?
> I should go to the old city, sir. Shall I give you a map?
> I should take a taxi, sir. Shall I get one for you?
> I should go to the lost property office, madam. Shall I show you the way?

6 Take the message

Listen to these guests and write down the message.

1 The guest's name is _____. He wants a table for _____ not _____ this evening.
2 The guest's name is _____. One of her guests: **a** is not coming. □ **b** wants a vegetarian meal. □ **c** will be late. □
3 The name of the company is _____. Their conference is from _____ to _____. They want seventeen _____ and thirty-two _____. They want meals for _____. How many conference rooms do they want? _____

7 Some conversations

Here is a conversation. Listen to the conversation and follow it in your book. Then rewind your cassette. Start the conversation again. This time, speak to the guest at the same time as the voice on the cassette.

RECEPTION: Good morning, Holiday Inn.
GUEST: I'm trying to contact Mr Vicini. Is he there?
RECEPTION: I'll try his room for you, madam. May I tell him who's calling?
GUEST: Yes, it's his wife.
RECEPTION: I'll try his room for you, madam . . . I'm afraid his line's engaged. Do you want to hold?
GUEST: No, just tell him to ring me as soon as possible, would you?
RECEPTION: Certainly, madam. I'll give him the message as soon as his line is free.

GUEST: Thank you.
RECEPTION: Thank you for calling, madam. Goodbye.
GUEST: Goodbye.

Now read these sentences. Then listen to this guest. Choose the sentence that best answers what the guest says. Say that sentence onto the cassette. You will then hear the right answer. Read the sentences now.

> I'm afraid there's no answer, sir. Shall I page him for you?
> Goodnight, sir.
> I'll put you through to his room, sir.
> At ten tomorrow morning, sir. I'll give him the message.

Now look at the next group of sentences. Then listen to the next guest. Again, choose the sentence that best answers what the guest says. Say that sentence onto the cassette. You will then hear the right answer. Read the sentences now.

> You're through now, Miss Roberts.
> Certainly, madam. May I tell him who's calling?
> There's a Miss Roberts on the line, Mr Brown. Do you wish to take the call?
> One moment, please. I'm putting you through now.

8 A letter

First read this letter. Use your dictionary.

Smith Plastics Inc.   2432 25th Avenue, Belmont 02178, Massachusetts, U.S.A.

The Marketing Manager,
Holiday Inn,
1–13–7 Hatchobori,
Chuo-ku,
Tokyo 104,
Japan.

Dear Mr Nashida,

With reference to our Tokyo Sales Conference last week, I regret to have to tell you that many of our delegates did not enjoy the food offered, particularly at the final banquet. We have received a number of complaints, some of them quite strong.

In the circumstance, I feel obliged to ask for some form of compensation, and look forward to hearing from you.

Yours sincerely,

A.J. Dutton

A. J. Dutton
Marketing Director

Now write a telex answering the letter. Use these words:

compensation	regret	feel	for	complaints	offered

```
THANK YOU _____ YOUR LETTER.  WE _____
TO HEAR THAT YOU HAVE RECEIVED _____ FROM YOUR
DELEGATES ABOUT THE FOOD _____ .  AS THE FOOD
WAS AGREED BY YOURSELVES, WE DO NOT _____ OBLIGED
TO OFFER ANY _____ .  LETTER FOLLOWS.
```

Now complete this letter. Use these words:

including	delegates	position	received	agreed	choice	obliged
regret	circumstances		compensation		understand	

Holiday Inn

YAESU

Dear Mr Dutton,

It was with _____ that we _____ your letter regarding your sales conference here.

May I point out that the menus were _____ by yourself, well in advance of the conference, and that your _____ had a _____ of food at each of the meals, _____ the final banquet.

In these _____ we do not feel _____ to offer _____ , and feel sure that you will _____ our _____ .

Yours sincerely,

Y. Nishida

Y. Nishida,
Marketing Manager

UNIT 6

Giving messages

Anita works in the Holiday Inn in Madrid. Sometimes her guests ask her to give messages to people who come to, or telephone, the hotel. Look at the pictures and words below. Then give the people the messages, like this:

CALLER: I wanted to speak to Mr Barbero.
ANITA: *He says he's ringing you tomorrow.*

ring/tomorrow

arrive/7.30

expect/lounge

come down/foyer

wait/bar

leave/tomorrow

send/fax

1 Has Mrs Smith arrived yet?

_____

2 Where can I find Miss Lopez?

_____

3 Is Mr Yamashta there?

_____

4 Do you know where Mr Robson is?

_____

5 Is Mr Kim still with you?

_____

6 I really do want to speak to Miss Uhlmann, you know.

2 More messages

Read the messages below.

1
From: MR. POPOV
To: MISS Svensson
Message:
meet/bar

2
From: Mrs Short
To: Mr Larkins
Message:
be late/this evening

3
From: Mr Hussein
To: Mr Said
Message:
call/tomorrow afternoon

4
From: Miss Andreotti
To: Mr Van der Houwe
Message:
expect/tomorrow morning/10

5
From: Mr Mohammed
To: Mr Singh
Message:
wait/restaurant

6
From: Miss Li
To: Mr Roberts
Message:
arrive/tomorrow evening

7
From: Mr Renard
To: Miss Porter
Message:
see/theatre

Now give the message to the person who asks for it, like this:

I *Hello, Miss Svensson. Mr Popov says he'll meet you in the bar.*

2 _____

3 _____

4 _____

5 _____

6 _____

7 _____

3 Saying you're sorry

Sometimes you have to apologise to people. Apologise to these people, like this:

My name's Jones. I was expecting Mr Smith to call me today.
I'm terribly sorry, Mr Jones. Mr Smith won't be able to call you today.

I My name's Laporte. I was hoping to meet Miss Garcia here this evening.

2 My name's Schmidt. I was expecting Mr Kreis to have dinner with me this evening.

3 My name's Pile. I was expecting Miss Ogden to go to the theatre tonight.

4 I was hoping Mrs Chan could stay an extra day. My name's Henderson.

5 My name's Loewenthal. Can you ask Mr Isaacs to attend a meeting this afternoon?

4 Who do you send?

Sometimes guests have problems. Look at what these guests say. Then say who you will send to their rooms to help them. Use these words:

waiter	porter	manager	electrician	plumber	*chambermaid*

GUEST: It's the bed. It hasn't been made.
YOU: *I'm very sorry, madam. I'll send the chambermaid immediately.*

I It's the TV. It won't work.

2 It's the tap. It won't turn on in the bath.

3 I asked for someone to collect my luggage twenty minutes ago.

4 All my jewels have been stolen.

5 I asked for dinner nearly an hour ago. Where is it?

Listen to these guests and write down the message.

Holiday Inn

1 FROM: Mr Smith

    FOR: Mrs Gabbiadini

    MESSAGE: He won't be able to _____ this _____. He's

               _____.

2 FROM: Mr Leadbetter

    FOR: Mr Abrahams

    MESSAGE: He's _____ in the _____.

3 FROM: Miss O'Malley

    FOR: Mrs Carmichael

    MESSAGE: She's been _____ at a _____. She'll be here

               at _____.

4 FROM: Mr Rodrigues

    FOR: Mr Kleist

    MESSAGE: He'll be here in _____.

5 FROM: Miss Sekiguchi

    FOR: Mr Macdonald

    MESSAGE: She's _____ you in the _____.

6 FROM: Mr Hindmarsh

    FOR: Mr Meier

    MESSAGE: _____ to call you this morning. He'll ring _____

               _____.

6   *Give the message*

 You have just written down some messages in Exercise 5. Now give the right messages to the people who ask for them. Say the message onto the cassette. You will then hear the right answer. Start each message with:

Hello, Mr (OR *Miss* OR *Mrs*) ... (the person's name).
And then:
I have a message for you.
Mr ... (the person's name) *says* ... (then the message).

7 Some conversations

Here is a conversation. Listen to the conversation and follow it in your book. Then rewind your cassette. Start the conversation again. This time, speak to the guest at the same time as the voice on the cassette.

GUEST: Excuse me, but there's something terribly wrong with my bill, you know, I'm quite certain of it.
CASHIER: I'm extemely sorry to hear that, sir. What seems to be the problem?
GUEST: It's the total for the bar. It seems far too high to me.
CASHIER: I'm fairly sure it's correct, sir. Would you like me to check it for you?
GUEST: I certainly would.
CASHIER: One moment, sir. I'll get the receipts.
GUEST: Fine.
. . .
CASHIER: I've checked your bill again, sir. I'm quite sure it's right.
GUEST: Let me see.
CASHIER: Here are the receipts, sir. They're all signed by you, as you can see. Would you like to check them yourself?
GUEST: Yes, I would.
. . .
GUEST: I'm so sorry. You're quite right.
CASHIER: It's no trouble, sir. How would you like to pay?
GUEST: By credit card. You take one . . .

Now read these sentences. Then listen to this guest. Choose the sentence that best answers what the guest says. Say that sentence onto the cassette. You will then hear the right answer. Read the sentences now.

> Here are your receipts, madam. This is your signature, isn't it? Room 409.
> Well, I'm fairly sure the bill's correct. Would you like to check it?
> I'm terribly sorry, madam. Can you see exactly what's wrong?
> Would you like me to check the receipts?

Now look at the next group of sentences. Then listen to the next guest. Again, choose the sentence that best answers what the guest says. Say that sentence onto the cassette. You will then hear the right answer. Read the sentences now.

> No, sir.
> One moment, sir. I'll see if Mr Brady left a message.
> May I have your name, sir?
> Certainly, sir.
> He says his wife has had an accident. At home. He's trying to phone the hospital.
> Yes, here we are, sir. I'm afraid Mr Brady won't be able to join you for dinner, sir.

First read this letter. Use your dictionary.

> 59 HIGH STREET
> BRACKLEY
> NORTHANTS
> NN13 5BA
>
> 10TH MARCH, 199—.
>
> DEAR SIR/MADAM
>
> I AM LOOKING FOR A HOTEL WHERE MY HUSBAND AND I CAN SPEND OUR HOLIDAYS FROM 1ST – 15TH AUGUST, 199—.
>
> UNFORTUNATELY, MY HUSBAND IS DISABLED, AND IS THEREFORE IN A WHEELCHAIR. HE CANNOT MANAGE STEPS, AND NEEDS SUITABLE WASHING FACILITIES.
>
> ARE YOU ABLE TO OFFER US SUITABLE ACCOMMODATION?
> I LOOK FORWARD TO HEARING FROM YOU.
>
> YOURS SINCERELY,
>
> A.J. HEDGES (MRS)

Now complete this letter. Use these words:

lifts	toilet	your	provisional	special	confirm	wheelchair
no	possible	of	cater	entrance	grateful	wide
		husband	disabled	which		

Dear Mrs Hedges,

Thank you for ———— letter ———— 10th March. We can certainly ———— for you and your ———— , as we have ———— bedrooms for the ———— . These have a ———— door into the bathroom, ———— is equipped with appropriate washing and ———— facilities.

There are ———— steps between the street and the ———— to the hotel, and the ———— are all wide enough to take a ———— .

I have made a ———— booking for you and your husband, and would be ———— if you could ———— it as soon as ———— .

Yours sincerely,

UNIT 7

1 Telling guests what to do

Look at these pictures and read the sentences. Then match the pictures with the correct sentence.

1 _____ 2 _____ 3 _____

4 _____ 5 _____ 6 _____

a Excuse me, sir. You mustn't leave your briefcase there. Someone may steal it.
b Excuse me, ladies. I must ask you to leave. That's the fire alarm.
c Excuse me, gentlemen. I must ask you to move. You're blocking the entrance.
d Excuse me, sir. You mustn't smoke here. It's a no smoking area.
e Excuse me, madam. You must complete the registration card. It's the law.
f Excuse me, sir. You must wait a moment. I'm seeing to this lady.

2 When you can't help

Sometimes you can't help a guest yourself. But you can tell them what they must do. Look at what these guests say and tell them what to do.

I'm	sorry afraid	I can't help you,	sir. madam.	You'll have to	go wait speak ring try	to the manager. him at his office. to the travel agent. another hotel. to the post office. until the next one comes.

1 Can you change these tickets for me, please?

_____

_____

2 Are you saying you haven't got a single free room?

_____

_____

3 But I need a taxi immediately.

_____

_____

4 I'm afraid I've lost my wallet, so I can't pay. What do you suggest I do?

_____

_____

5 Can you get me some stamps for the postcards, please?

_____

_____

6 But Mr Sanchez said he'd leave a message for me here.

_____

_____

3 *Helping the guest*

Look at what these guests say. Then use the sentences below to help the guest, like this:

GUEST: Where is Mr Dutton, do you know?
YOU: *If you like, I'll ring his room for you, madam.*

_____

If you follow the porter,	they'll be able to help you, sir.
If you like,	I'll see that she gets it, sir.
If you give me a message,	he'll show you the way, sir.
If you go out of the main entrance,	I'll book you a table, sir.
If you go to the boutique,	you'll find a taxi rank on your left, sir.

1 Where is room 310?

_____

2 Do you have a table for two free at eight?

_____

3 Miss Li isn't in her room. How can I contact her?

_____

4 Where can I get a taxi?

_____

5 Where can I get a present for my wife?

_____

44

Look at the messages these guests ask you to give to other people. Then pass the message, like this:

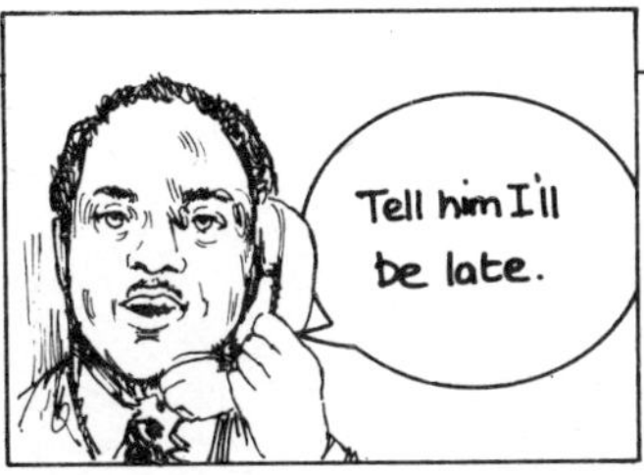

YOU: *He said he would be late, sir.*

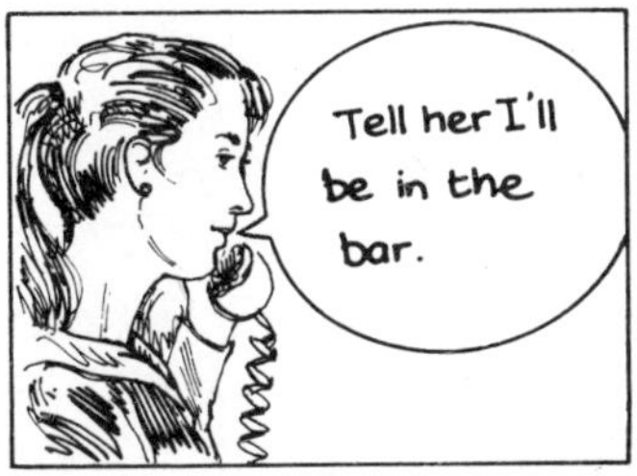

> Tell him I'll be late.

1 Tell her I'll be in the bar.

2 Tell her I'll meet her at 8.

3 Tell him I'll wait in the foyer.

4 Tell him I'll arrive at 7.30.

5 Tell him I'll be in the lounge.

6 Tell her I'll come down immediately.

1 _____
2 _____ 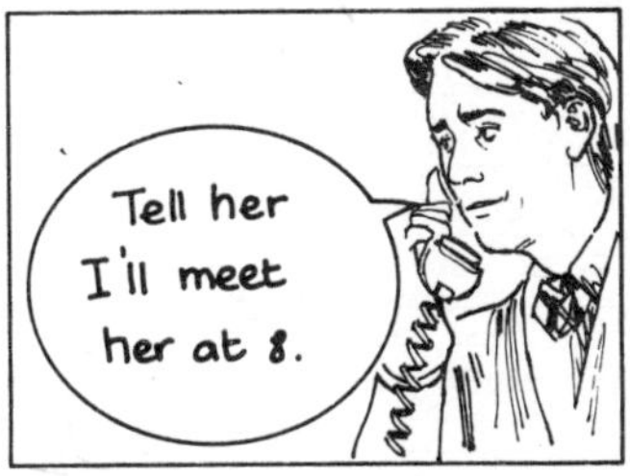
3 _____ 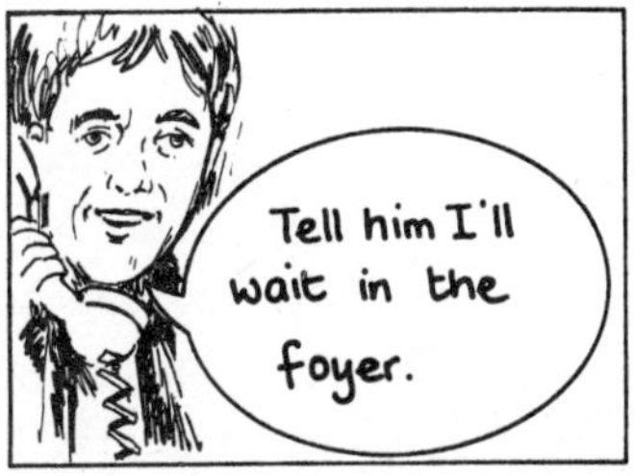
4 _____ 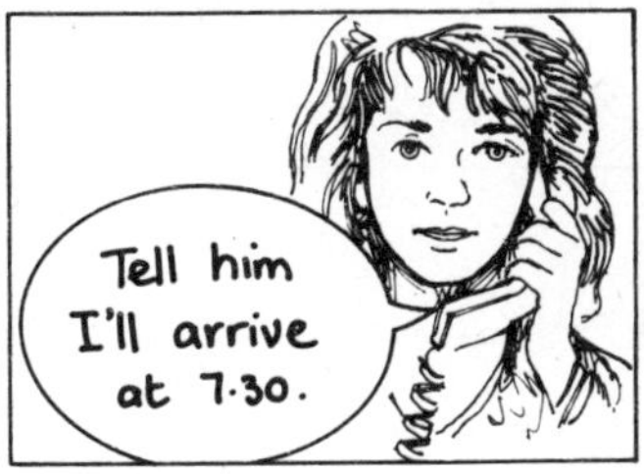
5 _____ 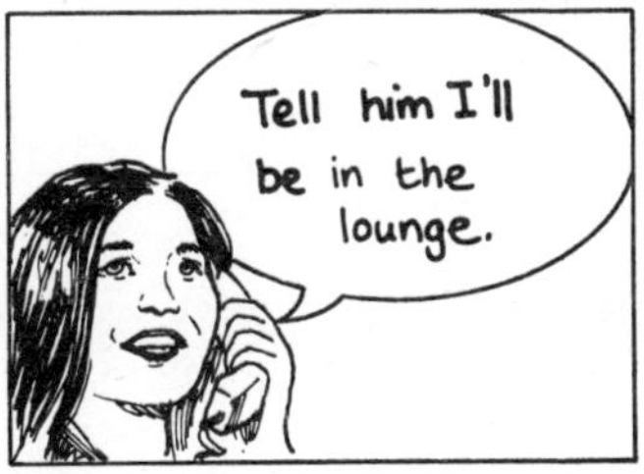
6 _____

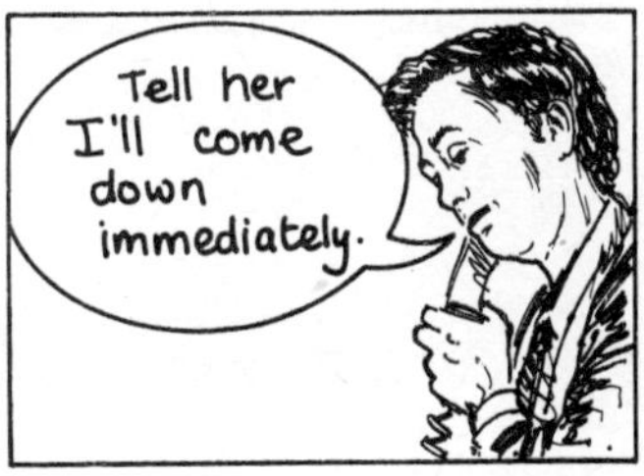

5 Take the message

Listen to these guests and write down the message.

Holiday Inn

1 Write down the telex

NUMBER: _____ANSWERBACK: _____

ATTENTION: _____

MESSAGE: _____

_____

_____

2 The guest's name is _____.

He wants to stay from _____ to _____ of _____.

3 The guests' name is _____.

They want to stay from _____ to _____.

They will arrive at about _____. They want a _____

and _____ food.

---

6 A conversation

Here is a conversation. Listen to the conversation and follow it in your book. Then rewind your cassette. Start the conversation again. This time, speak to the guest at the same time as the voice on the cassette.

RECEPTION: Good evening, madam, can I help you?

GUEST: I'm looking for a Mr Krishan. Do you know where I can find him?

RECEPTION: May I ask your name, madam?

GUEST: Cascarino.

RECEPTION: Ah yes, Miss Cascarino. Mr Krishan left a message for you. He said he would be about half an hour late.

GUEST: Oh dear. That's very inconvenient.

RECEPTION: If you like, I'll try his room for you.

GUEST: Yes, could you do that.

RECEPTION: If you could wait a moment, madam.

. . .

RECEPTION: No, I'm sorry, Miss Cascarino. I'm afraid there's no answer. I'm afraid you'll have to wait.

GUEST: Very well. Tell him I'll wait in the lounge for him.

RECEPTION: I'll do that.

7 Giving information

Look at the list of Holiday Inn hotels in your book. Sometimes guests want to transfer from one hotel to another, or want information about another hotel. Listen to these guests. Use the information in your book, and answer their questions. First, listen to this example and follow it in your book.

GUEST: Can you tell me, is there a hotel in Krakow?
RECEPTION: Yes, sir, there is.
GUEST: Can you give me the address?
RECEPTION: It's at seven Koniewa Street, three, zero, one, five, zero, Krakow.
GUEST: Can you spell that, please? The street name.
RECEPTION: Certainly, sir. It's K-O-N-I-E-W-A.
GUEST: And the telephone number?
RECEPTION: Zero, one, two. Then three, seven, five, zero, double four.
GUEST: Thank you very much.

Now here's the first guest. Use the information in your book, and the conversation to help you. Say your answers onto the cassette. You will then hear the right answer. Are you ready? Here's the first guest.

KRAKOW
7 Koniewa Street, 30150 Krakow
☎ (012) 37 50 44   Tx 2 25 356

ATHENS
50 Michalacopoulou Street, 11528 Athens
☎ (01) 724 83 22   Tx 218870

JEDDAH
Corniche Road, P.O. Box 10924, Jeddah 21443
☎ (02) 66 11 00   Tx 600755

BIRMINGHAM
Central Square, Birmingham B1 1HH
☎ (021) 631 2100   Tx 337272

MALTA
Tigne Street, Sliema
☎ Malta 34 11 73   Tx 1446

---

8 A letter

First read this letter. Use your dictionary.

> Dear Sir / Madam,
> My family and I would like to have our annual summer holiday in Madrid this year, and we are looking for a suitable hotel.
>
> Could you please send us details of your hotel, including distance from the airport, and your facilities.
>
> I look forward to hearing from you.
>
> Yours sincerely,
> G. Albertini
>
> G. Albertini (Mrs)

Now look at the information about the Holiday Inn, Madrid. Use this information to complete the letter below.

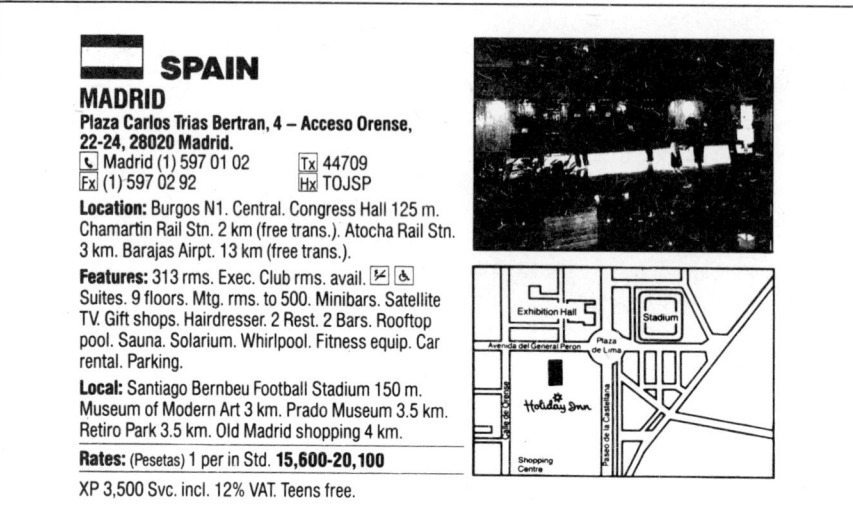

SPAIN

MADRID

Plaza Carlos Trias Bertran, 4 – Acceso Orense, 22-24, 28020 Madrid.

Madrid (1) 597 01 02   Tx 44709
Fx (1) 597 02 92   Hx TOJSP

Location: Burgos N1. Central. Congress Hall 125 m. Chamartin Rail Stn. 2 km (free trans.). Atocha Rail Stn. 3 km. Barajas Airpt. 13 km (free trans.).

Features: 313 rms. Exec. Club rms. avail. Suites. 9 floors. Mtg. rms. to 500. Minibars. Satellite TV. Gift shops. Hairdresser. 2 Rest. 2 Bars. Rooftop pool. Sauna. Solarium. Whirlpool. Fitness equip. Car rental. Parking.

Local: Santiago Bernbeu Football Stadium 150 m. Museum of Modern Art 3 km. Prado Museum 3.5 km. Retiro Park 3.5 km. Old Madrid shopping 4 km.

Rates: (Pesetas) 1 per in Std. **15,600-20,100**

XP 3,500 Svc. incl. 12% VAT. Teens free.

Holiday Inn

MADRID

Dear Mrs Albertini,

Thank you for your letter.

I enclose details of our hotel in Madrid. As you can see, our hotel is 13 _____ from Barajas _____ , but there is _____ _____ from the airport to the hotel.

We have 313 _____ , each of which is equipped with a _____ . We also have _____ television. The hotel has _____ shops, a _____ , two _____ and two _____ . We also have a _____ swimming _____   _____

The hotel is three kilometres from the Museum of _____ _____ and 3.5 kilometres from the _____ _____ .

If you have any further questions, please let me know.

Yours sincerely,

UNIT 8

1 Making requests

Look at these pictures and read the sentences. Then match the pictures with the sentences.

1 _____   2 _____   3 _____

4 _____   5 _____   6 _____

a Would you mind checking your bill, madam? It seems rather high.
b Would you mind waiting a moment, sir? I'm seeing to this lady.
c Would you mind filling in this card, sir? Then I'll give you your key.
d Would you mind moving, gentlemen? You're blocking the entrance.
e Would you mind following me, madam? I'll show you to your room.
f Would you mind coming with me, sir? I'll take you to the manager.

2 When do you start?

Look at the notice below. It tells you when your restaurant, cafeteria and bar open and close.

RESTAURANT	CAFETERIA
Breakfast *07.00 – 10.00* **Lunch** *12.00 – 14.00* **Dinner** *19.00 – 22.00*	**Open** *09.00 – 18.00* **BAR** **Open** *10.00 – 15.00* *17.00 – 02.00*

Now answer the guests' questions. Use the words *start* and *stop*, like this:

1 When does lunch begin?
We start serving at 12.00, sir/madam.

2 When does the bar close? At night?

_____

3 How early can I get breakfast?

_____

4 When does the restaurant shut? For dinner?

_____

5 How long does the cafeteria stay open?

_____

6 When does the bar open in the mornings?

_____

7 How soon can we get dinner?

_____

8 When does breakfast finish?

_____

3 *What do you say?*

Something is wrong with the guest's room. Say what you will have/get done about it, like this:

My bath is filthy, you know.
clean
I'll have/get it cleaned immediately, sir/madam.

1 The towels in my room are dirty.
change

_____

2 There are dirty ashtrays in my room. It's horrible.
remove

_____

3 The porter's left one of my suitcases downstairs.
bring

_____

4 Nobody has done anything about my bed.
make

_____

5 We're still waiting for our dinner. We asked room service for it half an hour ago.
send

_____

4 *What's wrong?*

Look at these pictures and the words below them. Then say what needs doing, like this:

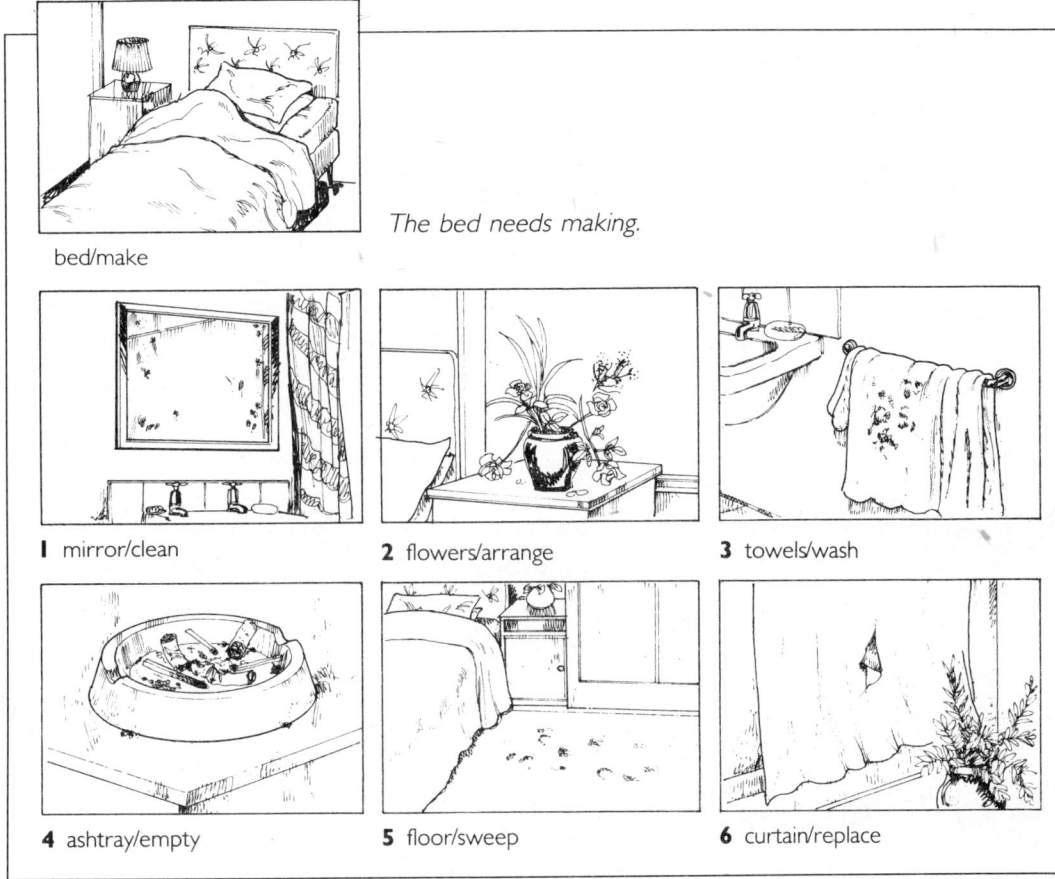

The bed needs making.

bed/make

1 mirror/clean   2 flowers/arrange   3 towels/wash

4 ashtray/empty   5 floor/sweep   6 curtain/replace

1 _____

2 _____

3 _____

4 _____

5 _____

6 _____

5 Take the message

Listen to these guests and write down the message.

Holiday Inn

1 The guest wants to hold a dinner for _____ people in a _____.
She wants a: **a** standard menu. ☐ **b** the chef's special menu. ☐ **c** their
own menu. ☐ The name is _____ and her phone number
is _____.

2 The guest's wife is _____. He wants a reservation from _____
to _____. His name is _____.

3 The guest is enquiring about a _____ service. She wants a _____
and another room _____ with _____ beds. She wants a
_____ in her room. She wants to stay from _____ to
_____ of _____ and her name is _____.

6 A conversation

Here is a conversation. Listen to the conversation and follow it in your book. Then
rewind your cassette. Start the conversation again. This time, speak to the guest at the
same time as the voice on the cassette.

GUEST: Good evening. I do hope you can help us. We had a reservation at the
             Grand, but when we went there just now, they said they had no record
             of the reservation.
RECEPTION: How many rooms do you want, madam?
GUEST: Two. A double room for me and my husband, and two single rooms for
             my son and daughter. And we also need a cot in our room for the baby.
             Can you manage that?
RECEPTION: Let me just check, madam. Would you mind waiting a moment?
GUEST: That's all right.
RECEPTION: Yes, we have two rooms, but they're on different floors. Does that
             matter?
GUEST: No, that'll be all right. And the cot?
RECEPTION: I'll see if we've got one spare. One moment, please ... Yes, we have. I'll
             get it sent to your room straightaway.
GUEST: Oh, thank you so much. That is a relief.

Look at these details of Holiday Inn hotels in England. Then turn on your cassette and listen to these guests. They are asking for information about these hotels. First, listen to this example and follow it in your book.

GUEST:	Can you tell me something about your hotel in Nottingham, please?
RECEPTION:	Certainly, sir. What would you like to know?
GUEST:	First, how far is it from the airport?
RECEPTION:	It's 20 kilometres, sir.
GUEST:	And does it have fitness equipment?
RECEPTION:	Yes, sir, it does.
GUEST:	And can I hire a car when I get there?
RECEPTION:	Yes, sir, you can.
GUEST:	Has it got facilities for the disabled?
RECEPTION:	Yes, sir, it has.
GUEST:	And finally, is there a bus service from the airport?
RECEPTION:	No, sir, I'm afraid there isn't.
GUEST:	I see. OK, thank you.

NOTTINGHAM GARDEN COURT
Castle Marina, Castle Boulevard, Nottingham.

Location: M1. Exits 25 or 26. Rail Stn. 1.5 km. East Midlands Airpt. 20 km.
Features: 100 rms. 4 floors. Mtg. rm. to 50. In-room movies. Satellite TV. 1 Rest. 1 Bar. Fitness equip. Tennis. Marina adj. Car rental. Free parking.
Local: Castle 1 km. Trent Bridge & Cricket 2 km. National Watersports Centre 8 km. Sherwood Forest 20 km.

Rates will be avail. six months before opening.

SLOUGH/WINDSOR
Ditton Road, Langley, Slough, Berks. SL3 8PT
Slough (0753) 44 244   Tx 848646
Fx (0753) 40 272   Hx LONSL
Location: Exit 5 off M4. Slough Rail Stn. 3 km. Heathrow Airpt. 6.5 km (free trans.).
Features: 302 rms. Suites. 6 floors. Mtg. rms. to 350. Minibars on request. In-room movies. Satellite TV. Gift shop. Hairdresser. 1 Rest. 1 Bar. Indoor pool. Sauna. Solarium. Whirlpool. Steambath. Massage. Fitness equip. Tennis. Table tennis. Car rental. Free parking. Children's playground.
Local: Windsor Castle. Safari Park. Madame Tussaud's Royalty & Empire Waxworks. Eton. Dorney Court. Runneymede. Marlow. Henley-on-Thames. Ascot race-course. Thames Valley – all within 15 km.

Rates: (Pounds Sterling) 1 per in Std. **76-89.50**

XP 15 Tax incl. Adv. dep. Teens free. SE.

PORTSMOUTH
North Harbour, Portsmouth, Hants. PO6 4SH.
Portsmouth (0705) 38 31 51   Tx 86611
Fx (0705) 38 87 01   Hx PTMUK
Location: M27 (500 m) exit 12. Havant Rail Stn. 6 km (free trans.). Southampton Airpt. 20 km (free trans.). Gatwick Airpt. 96 km. Heathrow Airpt. 112 km.
Features: 170 rms. Suites. 7 floors. Mtg. rms. to 300. In-room movies. Satellite TV. Gift shop. Health & Beauty Salon. 1 Rest. 1 Bar. Indoor pool. Sauna. Solarium. Whirlpool. Massage. Fitness equip. Squash. Table tennis. Car rental. Free parking. Terrace. Children's playground. Games room.
Local: Nr. Old Portsmouth. Seafront – Southsea resort. Historic Maritime attractions – HMS Victory, Mary Rose, Warrior. D-Day Museum. Sealife Centre. Isle of Wight. Porchester Castle. Marwell Zoo. New Forest.

Rates: (Pounds Sterling) 1 per in Std. **66-78**

XP 10 Tax incl. Teens free. SE.

NEWCASTLE-UPON-TYNE
Great North Road, Seaton Burn, Newcastle-upon-Tyne NE13 6BP.
Tyneside (091) 236 54 32   Tx 53271
Fx (091) 236 80 91   Hx NCLUK
Location: Adj. to A1. A6125/A1 Junction. Newcastle Airpt. 9 km (free trans.). Rail Stn. 12 km.
Features: 150 rms. Suite. 2 floors. Mtg. rms. to 300. In-room movies. Satellite TV. Gift shop. 1 Rest. 1 Bar. Indoor pool. Sauna. Solarium. Whirlpool. Fitness equip. Pool table & games room. Car rental. Free parking
Local: Coast 9 km. City centre and shopping 12 km. Hadrians Wall 13 km. Metro shopping centre and Garden Festival 1990 20 km. Beamish Museum 30 km. Bamburgh Castle 60 km.

Rates: (Pounds Sterling)
1 per in Std. **64** (up to 30.4.89) & **70** (from May 89)

XP 6 Tax incl. Teens free.

Now here's the first guest. Use the information in your book and the conversation to help you. Say your answers onto the cassette. You will then hear the right answer.

First read this letter. Use your dictionary.

Dear Sir/Madam,

My family and I would like to have our annual Holiday in London this year, and are looking for a suitable hotel near the city centre. We are also anxious that there should be some facilities for our children.

Could you please send me some details of your hotel, including distance from Heathrow airport and how to get to your hotel from there.

Please also let me know the details of the cost of double and single rooms.

Yours sincerely

M. Cascarino.

Now look at the information about the Holiday Inn at Marble Arch, London. Use the information to complete the fax on the next page. Also use these words:

equipped	from	such	also	rate card	attractions
courtesy	local	to	enjoy	details	cost

LONDON-MARBLE ARCH
134 George Street, London W1H 6DN.
☎ London (01) 723 12 77 Tx 27983
Fx (01) 402 06 66 Hx LONMA

Location: In city centre. Junction off Edgware Road/George Street. Nr. Marble Arch/Edgware Road Underground Stns. Paddington Stn. 2 km. Heathrow Airpt. 19 km.

Features: 241 rms. ⬚ ⬚ Suites. 12 floors. Mtg. rms. to 120. In-room movies. Satellite TV. Gift shop. 2 Rest. 1 Bar. Indoor pool. Sauna. Solarium. Whirlpool. Massage. Fitness equip. Car rental. Free parking.

Local: Close to Marble Arch, Oxford Street, Hyde Park and other local attractions, e.g. Buckingham Palace, museums, Madame Tussaud's.

Rates: (Pounds Sterling) 1 per in Std. **114-126.50**

XP 15 Tax incl. Teens free.

Holiday Inn
MARBLE ARCH

Dear Mrs Cascarino,

Thank you for your letter of . . .

Our hotel is —————— kilometres —————— Heathrow airport.
Although it does not say in the enclosed ——————, we run a
—————— bus from the airport —————— the hotel.

The hotel has an —————— pool, and —————— a whirlpool,
which I am sure your children would —————— . There are many
—————— —————— suitable for children, ——————
as Buckingham Palace and Madame Tussaud's.

There are also —————— movies and we are —————— with
satellite TV.

I enclose our —————— —————— showing details of the
—————— of rooms.

I look forward to hearing from you.

Yours sincerely

R J Buckminster

R J Buckminster
Reservations manager

UNIT 9

1 Giving advice

Look at these pictures and read the sentences. Then match the pictures with the sentences.

1 I still can't get through. _____

2 ...best way to the airport? _____

3 ...dinner this evening? _____

4 ...hairdresser? _____

5 ...local trips? _____

6 ...tennis? _____

a If I were you, I'd see our travel agent. They have all the details.
b If I were you, I'd make an appointment. Then you needn't wait.
c If I were you, I'd wait until morning. It's still very early in the States.
d If I were you, I'd book a court. It's a popular game with our guests.
e If I were you, I'd take a taxi. It's the quickest way.
f If I were you, I'd reserve a table. The restaurant can get very full.

2 Polite requests

Look at what these guests say. Then choose the best answer from the table below.

	tell me your room number,	I'll deposit them in our safe.
	give it to me,	I'll try and connect you.
	speak to the manager,	you'll see the taxi rank on your right.
	hold on,	I'll see if there are any.
If you'd like to	turn right by the lifts,	I'll get it faxed through for you.
	follow the porter,	he'll show you to your room.
	give them to me,	you'll find the bar down the corridor.
	go out of the main entrance,	I'll see if he's available.

1 I can't get through to that number in Germany.

_____

_____

2 Where can I get a taxi?

_____

_____

3 Where's the bar?

_____

_____

4 Is there somewhere safe you can keep my valuables?

_____

_____

5 I have a very serious complaint to make.

_____

_____

6 Where is my room? Number 310?

_____

_____

7 Where can I fax this information?

_____

_____

8 Are there any messages for me?

_____

_____

3 Answering questions

Look at these guests' questions. Then answer their questions, like this:

When does the swimming pool close?
five minutes
It will/It'll be closing in five minutes, madam.

1 When does the post go?
ten minutes

_____

2 When does the next bus leave?
quarter of an hour

_____

3 When does the manager arrive?
9 o'clock

_____

4 When does the swimming pool close?
twenty minutes

_____

5 When does the restaurant open?
half an hour

---

6 When does the cashier come?
8 o'clock

---

4 Asking questions

Look at what these guests say. Then ask them a question, like this:

Can I make a reservation?
When/arrive?
Certainly, sir. When will you be arriving?

I I'll have some extra guests for dinner.
How many/bring?

---

2 Tell Mr Carr I'll see him at eight.
Where/wait?

---

3 I'd like to settle my bill, please.
How/pay?

---

4 I've got to change my departure date.
When/leave?

---

5 I'm going on a weekend trip. Can you phone through any messages?
Where/stay?

---

5 Some conversations

Here is a conversation. Listen to the conversation and follow it in your book. Then rewind your cassette. Start the conversation again. This time, speak to the guest at the same time as the voice on the cassette.

GUEST: Good morning. Do you by any chance have a suite free today fortnight?
RECEPTION: If you'd like to hold the line a moment, sir, I'll check for you.
GUEST: Thank you.

. . .

RECEPTION: Hello?
GUEST: Yes?
RECEPTION: I'm very sorry, sir, we haven't got any free then.
GUEST: Oh, dear. Can you suggest anywhere else?
RECEPTION: If I were you, sir, I'd try the Grand.
GUEST: I'll do that. Thank you for your help.

GUEST:	A single room for two nights. Do you want a confirmation?
RECEPTION:	No, that's all right, madam. When will you be arriving?
GUEST:	Well, my train gets in just after six. I don't know how long it takes from the station. What's the best way to get to you?
RECEPTION:	If I were you, I'd take a taxi. It takes about ten minutes.
GUEST:	I'll do that.
RECEPTION:	We'll be expecting you about quarter past six, then, madam. Thank you for calling.

6 What do you say?

Look at the sentences below. Then turn on your cassette. Listen to what these guests say and choose the sentence that best answers the guest. Say the sentence onto the cassette. You will then hear the right answer.

> If I were you, madam, I'd deposit them in our safe.
> If I were you, sir, I'd book tickets in advance.
> If I were you, madam, I'd see the travel agent.
> If I were you, madam, I'd make an appointment.
> If I were you, madam, I'd take our courtesy bus.
> If I were you, sir, I'd go to the tourist information office.

7 Giving information

First look at this information about the Holiday Inn in Ljubljana, Yugoslavia.

★ YUGOSLAVIA

LJUBLJANA

Miklošičeva 3, 61000 Ljubljana.

Ljubljana (061) 21 14 34   Tx 31622
Hx LJBYU

Location: Central. Rail Stn. 700 m. Ljubljana-Brnik Airpt. 25 km (free trans.).

Features: 133 rms. Suites. 8 floors. Mtg. rm. to 50. Minibars. Satellite TV. Gift shop. Hairdresser. 1 Rest. 1 Bar. Indoor pool. Sauna. Massage. Fitness equip. Car rental. Free parking. Garden with bar during summer.

Local: Medieval Castle 1.5 km. Škofja Loka – 1000-year-old city 25 km. Postojna Caves 50 km. Skiing centres 50-100 km. Lipica with stud farm and riding school 90 km.

Rates: (German Marks) 1 per in Std. **140-165**

XP 50 Svc. & B'fast incl. SE.

Now answer these guests' questions about the hotel. Say your answers onto the cassette. You will then hear the right answer. Use: *Yes, sir/madam, we do.* OR *No, sir/madam, I'm afraid we don't.*

Now look at the information about the Holiday Inn in Casablanca, Morocco. Again answer the guests' questions. Say your answer onto the cassette. This time, use: *Yes, sir/madam, there is/are.* OR *No, sir/madam, I'm afraid there isn't/aren't.*

59

MOROCCO
CASABLANCA CROWNE PLAZA
Rond Point Hassan II, Casablanca.

☎ Casablanca 26 87 13/   Tx 22798
       22 35 27   Hx CASMO

Location: In the heart of the banking & business centre. Motorway Casablanca/Rabat, exit 4 km. Casa-port Rail Stn. 1.5 km. Mohammed V Airpt. 30 km.

Features: 180 rms. ⚌ ⚌ Suites. 16 floors. Mtg. rms. to 250. Minibars. In-room movies. Satellite TV. Gift shop. Hairdresser. 3 Rest. 2 Bars. Outdoor pool. Sauna. Solarium. Whirlpool. Steambath. Massage. Fitness equip. Disco. Car rental. Free parking.

Local: United Nations Square & musical fountain. Shopping of Mers Sultan. Souk of Habous 1.2 km. Old city – La Medina. Int'l fair site 3 km.

Rates: (Moroccan Dirhams) 1 per in Std. **700-800**

XP 200 Svc. incl. Teens free.

OPEN SPRING 1989

 A letter

First read this letter. Use your dictionary.

> Dear Sir/Madam,
>
> We are considering holding our annual conference in Munich this year, and therefore would like details of your facilities.
>
> Specifically, we need to know whether you can cater for 100 delegates, whether you have any sporting facilities and whether you have more than one restaurant and bar.
>
> Please also send details of your rates.
>
> Yours truly,
>
> *R. Dupont*
>
> R Dupont

Now look at these details of the Holiday Inn in Munich, Germany.

MUNICH LEOPOLDSTRASSE
Leopoldstrasse 194, 8000 Munich 40.

☎ Munich (089) 38 17 90   Tx (17) 897930
Fx (089) 361 71 19   Hx MUCLS

Location: Motorway Frankfurt/Nürnberg/Salzburg, exit Schwabing. Rail Stn. 5 km. Munich-Riem Airpt. 14 km.

Features: 364 rms. ⚌ Suites. 7 floors. Mtg. rms. to 600. Minibars. Gift shop. 2 Rest. 2 Bars. Indoor pool. Sauna. Solarium. Massage. Fitness equip. Disco. Car rental. Parking. Beer garden. Terrace.

Local: BMW Museum 1 km. Olympic Park and Olympia Stadium 1.5 km. Theatres 2.5 km. Opera 5 km. Museums 8-10 km. Schleissheim Castle 12 km.

Rates: (German Marks) 1 per in Std. **215-260**

XP 25 Tax & Svc. incl. Teens free. SE.

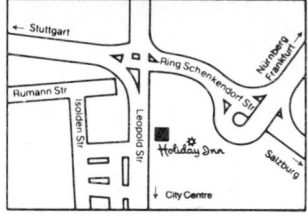

Now use this table to answer the letter. Remember to answer Mr Dupont's questions according to the information given above. There is only one right answer. Write your letter on a piece of paper.

Thank you for your	letter postcard telex fax	of ...

We can certainly cater for I'm afraid we cannot cater for	100 delegates as we	only have have

364 150	bedrooms. Our meeting rooms	cannot hold can hold	more than up to	600.

As regards sporting facilities	we only have an indoor pool. we have everything you want. we have an indoor pool and fitness equipment, but unfortunately no tennis courts.

I enclose full details of the services we can offer and also of I regret we cannot help you.	our rates. places of local interest.

UNIT 10

In this last Unit, practise what you have learnt!

1 *Some conversations*

Look at the sentences below. Then turn on your cassette. Listen to what these guests say and choose the sentence that best answers the guest. Say the sentence onto the cassette. You will then hear the right answer.

Would you like to fill in the registration card, please?

One moment, madam. I'll check.

Good evening, madam. May I help you?

There's one on the desk there, madam.

Yes, that's right. A single room with shower for three nights.

It's 472 3981.

If I were you, sir, I'd try the Europa. Would you like their telephone number?

Not at all, sir. I'm sorry we can't help you.

I'm very sorry, sir. I'm afraid we're full tonight.

Holiday Inn, can I help you?

Yes, sir, we do. We've got a swimming pool and a playground. We also have a games room.

I'll reserve those rooms for you, sir. Can you tell me your name?

Certainly, sir. What would you like to know?

Thank you very much, sir. Goodbye.

Holiday Inn, good evening.

There's TV in every room, sir. We've got satellite TV as well.

Mr Smith. Would you mind confirming this, sir?

We run a courtesy bus every half hour, sir.

Certainly, sir. How many rooms would you like? And when will you be arriving?

Yes, sir, you can.

2 What do you say?

Look at these pictures and read the sentences. Then match the pictures with the sentences.

...railway station?	...speak to Mr Aziz?	
1 _____	2 _____	3 _____
...dirty ashtrays.	...restaurant?	...bill please.
4 _____	5 _____	6 _____

a Would you mind filling in this card, madam?
b Certainly, madam. How will you be paying?
c It's situated on the first floor, madam.
d If I were you, I'd take a taxi. It's the easiest way.
e I'll have them taken away immediately, sir.
f If you'd like to hold on, I'll see if he's in his room.

3 A telex

Complete this telex. Use these words:

thanks	reservation	enquiry	follows	for	regards	confirm	to

```
MANY _____ FOR YOUR _____ ABOUT TWO

DOUBLE ROOMS _____ THE NIGHTS OF 20TH

_____ 30TH AUGUST.  WE _____

YOUR _____ , LETTER _____ .

_____

T. SEKIGUCHI
```

Now complete this letter. Use these words.

playground	look forward	for	also	holidays	run	see	journey
about	suggest	facilities	brochure	early	enclose	full	sincerely
			courtesy				

Holiday Inn

LEOPOLDSTRASSE

Dear Mr Robinson,

Thank you ———————— your enquiry ———————— the
———————————— our hotel can offer for family —————————— .

I ———————— our ————————— , from which you will
———————————— that we have a games room, a children's ——————————
and ————————— a swimming-pool.

We ————————— a ————————— bus to and from the airport. The
————————— takes about 20 minutes.

I ————————— you make an ————————— reservation, as we are
often very ————————— during the months of July and August.

I ————————— ————————— to hearing from you.

Yours ——————————

H. J. Kleist (Mrs)

5 Take the message

 Listen to these guests and write down the message.

1 The guest's name is ——————. She'll be arriving on ——————
   and will be staying until ——————.

2 The guest's room number is ——————. He wants you to tell
   —————— that he will wait in the ——————. The gentleman
   will be arriving at about ——————.

3 Mr —————— wants you to tell Mrs —————— he will be
   —————— minutes late because of a ——————.

4 The guest wants a room on the —————— —————— because her
   husband is ——————.

5 The guest wants to hold a company ——————. The date is ——————.
   There will be —————— guests. He wants you to send him sample
   ——————. He also wants a —————— ——————.

6 The guest's name is ——————. He wants a table for ——————
   at —————— o'clock. He wants to sit ——————.

7 The guest's name is ——————. She wants a —————— room
   and two —————— ——————. She also wants a ——————
   in the —————— ——————.
   The guest will arrive on —————— and stay until ——————.

8 The number is —————— and the country ——————. The
   answerback is ——————. The telex is for the attention of ——————.
   The message reads ————————————————————
   ————————————————————————————
   ————————————————————————————
   ————————————————————————————
   ——————————————
   ——————————————

Now complete this fax. Use these words:

be able to	bedrooms	cater	will be hearing	in	your
	sent	regret	conference		

SENT BY: XEROX Telecopier 7017; 17/08/90 ; 9:01 ; 0044 089 38 1790

LEOPOLDSTRASSE

Dear Miss Dupont,

Thank you for _____ letter of 15th April.

I _____ we cannot _____ for your annual sales _____ as we do not have the two hundred _____ you require.

However, the Holiday Inn hotel _____ Frankfurt would _____ meet your _____ , and I have _____ your letter on to the Manager.

I am sure you _____ from him soon.

Yours truly,

M. Schneider

M. Schneider

Now complete this letter. Use these words:

cater	sample	particularly	in	satisfactory	requested
details	sporting	facilities	relaxing	delegates	changed

Holiday Inn

VELIZY

Dear Mr Renard,

To confirm our telex of 15th June, we can certainly _____ for your conference _____ January next year. I enclose full _____ of our _____ , which I hope you will find _____ .

I _____ draw your attention to our _____ facilities, which I am sure many of your _____ will find useful and _____ .

As _____ , I enclose _____ menus for your consideration. These can, of course, be _____ should you wish.

Yours sincerely,

N. Flamand.

Look at the information about these three Holiday Inn hotels. Then turn on your cassette. Some guests are asking questions about these hotels. Use the information and answer their questions. Use these phrases:

> Yes, there is./No, I'm afraid there isn't.
> Yes, there are./No, I'm afraid there aren't.
> Yes, we do./No, I'm afraid we don't.
> Yes, you can./No, I'm afraid you can't.
> Yes, we have./No, I'm afraid we haven't.

KUALA LUMPUR – ON THE PARK
P.O. Box 10983, Jalan Pinang,
50732 Kuala Lumpur, West Malaysia.
KL (03) 248 10 66   Tx 30239
Fx (03) 243 59 30   Hx KULMY

Location: In city centre. Subang Int'l Airpt. 25 km.

Features: 200 rms. Suites. 12 floors. Mtg. rm. to 150. Minibars. In-room movies. Gift shop. Hairdresser. 4 Rest. 1 Bar. Outdoor pool. Sauna. Fitness equip. Tennis. Children's playground. Business services.

Local: Handicraft Centre 1.5 km. Shopping 2 km. Chinatown 4 km. Central Market 4 km.

Rates: (Malaysian Ringgit) 1 per in Std. **130-150**
Adv. dep. Teens free.

SINGAPORE – ROYAL
25 Scotts Road, Singapore 0922.
737 79 66   Tx 21818
Fx 737 66 46   Hx SINSN

Location: In the heart of the city's most exciting entertainment & shopping district. Changi Int'l Airpt. 25 km.

Features: 600 rms. Suites. 15 floors. Mtg. rms. to 350. Minibars. In-room movies. Satellite TV. Gift shops. Hairdresser. 3 Rest. 2 Bars. Outdoor pool. Sauna. Steambath. Massage. Fitness equip. Car rental. Parking.

Local: Shopping complex. Embassies. Rest. Theatre.

Rates: (Singapore $) 1 per in Std. **130-145** Teens free.

PAKISTAN
ISLAMABAD   Aga Khan Road,
Shalimar 5, P.O. Box 1251, Islamabad.
Islamabad (051) 82 61 21   Tx 5612 & 5740
Fx (051) 82 06 48   Hx RWPPK

Location: Nr. embassies, government secretariats. Int'l Airpt. 23 km (free trans. on adv. request).

Features: 300 rms. Suites. 5 floors. Mtg. rms. to 600. Minibars. In-room movies. Satellite TV. Gift shops. Hairdresser. 2 Rest. Indoor pool. Fitness equip. avail. Tennis. Squash. Table tennis. Golf. Horse-riding. Badminton.

Local: Faisal Mosque 3 km. Jasmine Gardens 8 km.

Rates: (Pakistani Rupee) 1 per in Std. **1,800**
7.5% Tax. Adv. dep. Teens free.

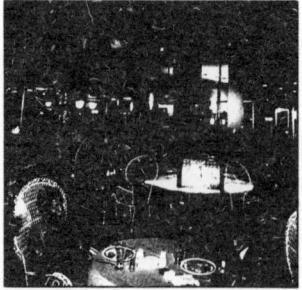

KEY TO EXERCISES

Unit 1

1 WHAT DO THEY DO?

2 She's a waitress.
3 She's a receptionist.
4 He's a porter.
5 She's a cashier.
6 He's a barman.
7 She's a maid.
8 He's a lift attendant.
10 The waitress works in the restaurant. She serves the meals.
11 The receptionist works at the front desk. She welcomes the guests.
12 The porter works all over the hotel. He carries the luggage.
13 The cashier works at the front desk. She prepares the bills.
14 The barman works in the bar. He serves the drinks.
15 The maid works in the bedrooms. She cleans them.
16 The lift attendant works in the lift. He takes guests to the right floor.

2 THE GRAND HOTEL

1 It has (OR It's) got a lift.
2 It has (OR It's) got television in the rooms.
3 It has (OR It's) got showers in the rooms.
4 It has (OR It's) got toilets in the rooms.
5 It has (OR It's) got air conditioning.
6 It has (OR It's) got telephones in the rooms.
7 It has (OR It's) got a restaurant with three stars.
8 It hasn't (OR It has not) got a tennis court.
9 It hasn't (OR It has not) got a swimming pool.
10 It has (OR It has not) got garage parking.
11 It hasn't (OR It has not) got conference facilities.

3 WHAT DO YOU SAY?

2 b **3** e **4** a **5** f **6** c

4 TELL THE GUEST THE WAY

1 Certainly, madam. Turn *right out of* the hotel. At the *crossroads, turn* right and the *cinema* is *on* your right.
2 *Certainly, sir/madam. Turn left out of the hotel. At* the crossroads, *turn* left. When you reach the junction, *cross* the road and the disco is *on your* left.
3 Certainly, sir. Turn left *out of* the hotel. At the *crossroads,* turn *right.* Go straight on and at the *junction,* turn right. The theatre is *on* your right.
4 *Certainly,* madam. *Turn left out of the hotel. At* the crossroads, go *straight* on and the museum *is on your left.*
5 Certainly, madam. Turn right out of the hotel. At *the crossroads, turn right* and *the travel agent is on your left.*
6 *Certainly, sir/madam. Turn left out of the hotel.* At the *crossroads, turn right.* Go *straight* on and when you come to the *junction,* turn *left.* It's *on your left.*

 ### 5 WHAT DOES THE GUEST WANT?

Tapescript

Sally works at the reception desk in a hotel. A lot of guests ask her questions. Listen to the question. Then read the answers in your book. Listen to the question again, and put a tick against the right answer. Here's number 1.

I want to go to the station. Can you get me a taxi immediately, please?

Number 2

I'm trying to contact a friend of mine, a Mr G. Smith. His address is Station Road, but I don't know the number. Can you find out his telephone number, please?

Number 3

SALLY: Royal Hotel, good afternoon.
GUEST: Good afternoon. Have you got a double room and two single rooms free for tonight? For three nights, actually.
SALLY: One moment, sir, I'll check.

Number 4

SALLY: Royal Hotel, good evening.
GUEST: I want to book a table for two in your restaurant for tomorrow night, please.
SALLY: One moment, sir, I'll put you through.

Number 5

GUEST: Excuse me, can I borrow a pen so I can fill in this registration form?
SALLY: Certainly, madam.

Key

1 b   2 a   3 c   4 b   5 c

6   TAKE THE MESSAGE

Tapescript

Listen to these guests. They are asking you to take a message. Listen to what they say and write down the message.

Number 1

RECEPTION: Royal Hotel, good evening.
CALLER: Good evening. Can you give a message to Mr Sato in room four thirty-three, please.
RECEPTION: Certainly, sir.
CALLER: My name's Smith. That's S-M-I-T-H. Tell Mr Sato I'm arriving at seven thirty, not seven o'clock.
RECEPTION: Right, sir.

Number 2

RECEPTION: Royal Hotel, good afternoon.
CALLER: My name's Al Said Al Saba'a. My flight is late, but please keep my room for me. I'm arriving at about ten o'clock tonight.
RECEPTION: Certainly, sir.

Number 3

RECEPTION: Reception.
GUEST: Hello. This is room 42. There's something wrong with the television in my room. It doesn't work. Can someone come and fix it, please?
RECEPTION: Of course, sir.

Number 4

GUEST: Is that reception?
RECEPTION: Yes, madam.
GUEST: I'm in room three oh one. The room's dirty, the bed hasn't been made and the ashtrays are full. It's disgraceful.
RECEPTION: I'll send someone at once, madam.

Number 5

RECEPTION: May I help you, sir?

GUEST: Yes, my name's Leclerc. I'm in room 77. I'm expecting a Mr Milewski. When he arrives, can you tell him I'm in the West Bar?

RECEPTION: Yes, sir.

Number 6

RECEPTION: Reception.

GUEST: I've got to leave tomorrow morning, rather than in the afternoon. Can you change my flight booking, or do I need to go to a travel agent?

Key

1 Mr Sato. Mr Smith, arriving at 7.30.
2 Keep his room. 10 p.m. (22.00).
3 The television doesn't work.
4 The maid.
5 The West Bar. Room 77.
6 Tomorrow morning. His flight booking.

8 A FAX

Thank you for your *letter* of 3rd March.

I am pleased to *confirm* your *reservation* for two *single rooms* and one *double room* from 5th–10th August, 199–.

We *look forward to* welcoming you on 5th August.

9 A TELEX

1 a 2 b 3 d 4 a

Unit 2

1 WHAT DO YOU SAY?

1 d 2 f 3 b 4 c 5 a 6 e

2 ASKING QUESTIONS

1 How 2 What 3 When 4 Where 5 Where 6 What 7 Who 8 How
9 Who 10 When

3 ANSWERING QUESTIONS

1 It leaves from the main entrance.
2 It opens at 11.30 in the morning.
3 It closes at 5.30 in the afternoon.
4 We take most credit cards.
5 We don't allow dogs, I'm afraid.
6 We don't charge for making travel arrangements.
7 They run every half hour.
8 We sell toilet articles in our shop.
9 We don't accept personal cheques, I'm afraid.
10 It costs eighteen marks.

4 ANSWER THE GUESTS' QUESTIONS

2 waited, left 3 closed 4 went 5 took 6 ordered 7 put 8 reserved, asked
9 cleaned 10 booked, asked

5 ASKING THE GUEST QUESTIONS

2 did you make 3 did you lose 4 did you speak 5 did you settle

6 SAYING *NO* POLITELY

2 No, sir/madam, I'm sorry. I'm afraid we didn't receive it.
3 No, sir/madam, I'm sorry. I'm afraid we didn't find it.
4 No, sir/madam, I'm sorry. I'm afraid we didn't manage to book them.
5 No, sir, I'm sorry. I'm afraid we didn't know (that).

 ## 7 THE REGISTRATION CARD

✱ Holiday Inn®

REGISTRATION CARD

ROOM NUMBER	ARR DATE	DEP DATE	ADULT	CHILD	RATE	CODE Nº
322, 323	18·7	25·7	2	2		

PRINT BLOCK LETTERS ONLY PLEASE

SURNAME _PHILLIPS_

FORENAME _ANTHONY_

PRIVATE ADDRESS _17 ACACIA ROAD, DAVENTRY, ENGLAND_

COMPANY NAME & ADDRESS _____

OCCUPATION _TEACHER_

NATIONALITY _BRITISH_   PASSPORT Nº _605791 T_

CAR REG. Nº _E 674 WWL_   NEXT DESTINATION _HOME_

MY ACCOUNT WILL BE SETTLED BY

☐ CASH   ☐ CHEQUE *   ☐ COMPANY ACCOUNT *

☐ AMERICAN EXPRESS   ☐ DINERS CLUB   ☐ VISA   ☒ ACCESS

☐ OTHER C/C   * BY PRIOR ARRANGEMENT

SPECIMEN SIGNATURE   CLERK'S INITIALS

A. Phillips

MPL 94

Tapescript

Karen works in the Holiday Inn, Frankfurt. Listen to her registering a British family. As you listen, fill in the registration card in your book.

KAREN: Good evening, sir, may I help you?
GUEST: Hello. My name's Phillips. I reserved two rooms for my wife and family.
KAREN: Ah, yes, Mr Phillips. Here we are. Shall I complete the registration card for you?
GUEST: Thank you. The name's Phillips. P-H-I-double L-I-P-S.
KAREN: And what is your forename, sir, your first name?
GUEST: Anthony. A-N-T-H-O-N-Y.

KAREN: And your private address, sir?
GUEST: 17 Acacia Road, Daventry, England.
KAREN: I'm sorry, sir. How do you spell that?
GUEST: 17 Acacia, A-C-A-C-I-A Road. Then D-A-V-E-N-T-R-Y, Daventry, England.
KAREN: And what is the name of your company, sir?
GUEST: I haven't got one. We're here on holiday. I'm a teacher.
KAREN: Right, sir. Teacher. And you're British, I take it, sir.
GUEST: Yes, that's right.
KAREN: What is your passport number, sir?
GUEST: One moment. Ah, it's 6-oh-5-7-9-1-T.
KAREN: Do you have a car here, sir?
GUEST: Yes. It's number E-6-7-4-W-W-L.
KAREN: And where will you be going next, sir?
GUEST: After this? Home.
KAREN: And finally, sir, how do you intend to pay?
GUEST: By credit card. Access.
KAREN: That's fine, sir. Now, we've put you in rooms 322 and 323. You've arrived today, the 18th July. How long are you staying with us?
GUEST: A week. We're going on the 25th.
KAREN: Fine, sir. And it's two adults and two children?
GUEST: That's right.
KAREN: Thank you very much, sir. I'll get the porter to show you to your rooms now. I hope you enjoy your stay with us.

 8 TAKE THE MESSAGE

Tapescript

Listen to these guests and write down what they want you to do. Here's the first guest.

GUEST: Is that reception?
RECEPTION: Yes, madam, can I help you?
GUEST: This is room 456. It's the tap in the bathroom. It's dripping. Can someone come and fix it?
RECEPTION: Certainly, madam. I'll send someone at once.

Number 2
GUEST: Is that the Holiday Inn?
RECEPTION: Yes, sir. How can I help you?
GUEST: I'd like to book a single room, please. With shower. From the 14th of March to the 18th. Have you got a room free then?
RECEPTION: Yes, we have, sir. Can you give me your name?
GUEST: Larrosa. L-A-double R-O-S-A.
RECEPTION: And your address...

Number 3
RECEPTION: Reception.
GUEST: Look, could you give a message to Mr Al Ruwahi? That's A-L and then R-U-W-A-H-I. Tell him I can't come this evening. My wife's very ill. Tell him I'm very sorry, and I'll phone him tomorrow. Oh, he's in room five double two.
RECEPTION: I'll give him the message, sir.
GUEST: Thank you. My name's Kreis. K-R-E-I-S.

Number 4
RECEPTION: Reception.
GUEST: Can you tell Miss Temple in room 352 that she should take a taxi this evening? I can't come and collect her, as I said. Tell her to take a taxi to the Tang, T-A-N-G, Chinese restaurant in the city centre, to arrive at eight this evening.
RECEPTION: Certainly, sir. Thank you.

Number 5

RECEPTION: Holiday Inn, good afternoon.
GUEST: I'm calling from the States. Can you get me Mr Marchant?
RECEPTION: I'm afraid Mr Marchant is out, sir. Can I give him a message?
GUEST: Sure. Tell him to ring Jones, J-O-N-E-S, immediately he gets in, on 617 4563890. It's urgent.
RECEPTION: I'll see he gets the message, sir.

Number 6

GUEST: I'd like you to send some flowers to my room, please. Before seven o'clock this evening. I don't mind what they are, but say about 50 marks worth. Room 103.
RECEPTION: I'll order them straightaway, sir.

Key

1 456. The tap is dripping.
2 Larrosa. Single room with shower. 14th–18th March.
3 Mr Al Ruwahi; 522; Kreis; can't come this evening; his wife is very ill; sorry; phone tomorrow.
4 Miss Temple, room 352. Tang Chinese restaurant. 8.
5 Jones, USA (States), 617 4563890.
6 Flowers. 103. About 50 marks.

10 A FAX

Thank you *for* your letter of 1st May.

I *regret* our accommodation is fully *booked* for the *period* 1st–4th July. I am afraid we cannot therefore *help* you in this instance. May I *suggest* you *try* to *get* a reservation in our other hotel in Frankfurt? I enclose our hotel directory showing the *address*.

We *hope* you will stay with us the next time you come to Frankfurt.

Yours sincerely,

11 A TELEX

REGRET WE ARE *UNABLE* TO ACCEPT YOUR *RESERVATION* FOR 15TH MARCH AS WE ARE *FULLY BOOKED*. I *SUGGEST* YOU TRY OUR *OTHER* HOTEL IN FRANKFURT, TELEX NUMBER 411805.

REGARDS

Unit 3

1 ASKING QUESTIONS

1 d 2 b 3 f 4 a 5 e 6 c

2 SOME MORE QUESTIONS

1 Has your guest arrived, sir/madam?
2 Have you looked in the bar, sir/madam?
3 Have you ordered a taxi, sir/madam?
4 Have you collected all your luggage, sir/madam?
5 Have you seen our information booklet, sir/madam?
6 Have you left it in your room, sir/madam?

3 WHAT'S THE BEST ANSWER?

1 I've told the chef to prepare her meals specially, sir.
2 I've reserved a room overlooking the lake, madam.
3 I've given her your message, madam.

4 I've changed your flight to AF 345, sir.
5 I've ordered it for 6.30, sir.
6 I've sent them up to your room, sir.

4 SOME SHORT ANSWERS

1 No, sir/madam, I'm afraid I haven't.
2 No, sir/madam, I'm afraid it hasn't.
3 No, sir/madam, I'm afraid they haven't.
4 No, sir/madam, I'm afraid I haven't.
5 No, madam, I'm afraid he hasn't.
6 No, sir/madam, I'm afraid it hasn't.

5 HE MAY HAVE GONE TO THE BAR

1 I don't know, sir. She may/could have gone to the restaurant.
2 I don't know, sir/madam. He may/could have left the hotel.
3 I don't know, sir/madam. She may/could have decided to go out.
4 I don't know, sir/madam. My colleague may/could have taken it to the cloakroom.
5 I don't know, sir/madam. She may/could have stayed in her room.
6 I don't know, sir/madam. He may/could have cancelled his reservation.

6 TALKING TO GUESTS

1 someone/somebody   **2** anything   **3** no one/nobody   **4** nothing
5 somewhere   **6** anyone   **7** something   **8** nowhere   **9** anywhere

7 AT THE CASHIER'S

Tapescript

Christine works as a cashier in the Holiday Inn, Paris. Listen to these guests asking her questions. Then read the answers in your book. Listen to the question again and put a tick against the right answer.

Number 1

Excuse me, can I change some American dollars into francs? I don't want to change the German marks, I'll need them.

Number 2

What's your exchange rate for the Japanese yen?

Number 3

Can I cash this traveller's cheque with you? I'd like half in lire, half in pesetas, if that's all right, but the cheque's in dollars.

Number 4

Can I pay my bill by credit card? I haven't got enough cash, and I don't want to use my traveller's cheques.

Number 5

I'm sorry, there seems to be something wrong with my bill. There's an item here, cigarettes from the bar, but I'm a non-smoker. The restaurant bill's OK, but could you check that one item?

Key

1 a   **2** c   **3** b   **4** b   **5** c

8 TAKE THE MESSAGE

Tapescript

Listen to these guests and write down what they want you to do. Here's the first guest.

Tapescript

My flight from Chicago has been cancelled because of the weather, and I've got a room booked with you for four nights starting today. I can get another flight tomorrow, but can you keep the room for me? I'll get to you tomorrow evening.

Number 2

I'm afraid I've just upset the dinner trolley in my room. Could someone come and clear up the mess? I really am very sorry about this.

Number 3

This is room two-oh-one, Mitsui, M-I-T-S-U-I speaking. I'm expecting a call from Japan, from a Mr Ito. When he calls at around six, could you tell him I've gone out? I'll call him at around seven. Today, that is, not tomorrow.

Certainly sir. I'll tell Mr Ito when he calls.

Number 4

We're looking for somewhere to hold a sales conference next October. Can you send me details of your facilities and your prices?

Certainly, madam. Could you give me the name . . .

Key

1 cancelled; keep his room; tomorrow evening.
2 c
3 Mitsui; 201; 6; b
4 sales conference; facilities; prices

9 SOME CONVERSATIONS

Now read the sentences in your book. Then listen to this guest. Choose the sentence that best answers what the guest says. Say that sentence onto the cassette. You will then hear the right answer. Read the sentences now.

Now here's the guest. Are you ready?

GUEST: Good afternoon.
YOU: Good afternoon, madam. What can I do for you?
GUEST: I'd like to cash this traveller's cheque, please.
YOU: How much is the cheque for, madam?
GUEST: It's for a hundred pounds. What's the exchange rate, by the way?
YOU: It's ten francs to the pound.
GUEST: So that's a thousand francs.
YOU: That's right, madam. Here you are, and thank you.

Now look at the next group of sentences. Then listen to the next guest. Again, choose the sentence that best answers what the guest says. Say that sentence onto the cassette. You will then hear the right answer. Read the sentences now.

GUEST: Morning.
YOU: Good morning, sir.
GUEST: I'd like my bill, please.
YOU: Certainly, sir. What's your room number?
GUEST: Room double three one.
YOU: One moment, sir. Here it is. How would you like to pay?
GUEST: By credit card.
YOU: That'll be fine, sir.
GUEST: Hey, what's this? I didn't buy any cigarettes. I'm a non-smoker.

YOU: Let me just check. Oh, I am sorry, sir. This receipt has been put in the wrong place. It's for room double three two.

GUEST: Well, can you take it off my bill?

YOU: Yes, of course, sir. One moment, please, and I'll change it.

GUEST: Thank you.

10   A LETTER

Dear Miss Langan,

Thank you very much for your *enquiry* of 16th February.

As you will see from the enclosed brochure, our hotel is a large, *modern* one right in the city centre. *Transport* to and from the airport is easy, as we run our own free bus *service* every half hour.

Our *facilities* for conferences are, we like to think, *excellent*. We can accommodate *groups* of 20 to 100, as we *have got* four conference rooms of different *sizes* in the hotel.

Each room *has got* its own shower, television and mini bar to make our guests' *stay* as *comfortable* as possible.

For groups of more than 50, we are pleased to *quote* a special *rate*. Perhaps you can let me know how many representatives of your company there will be, so that I may send you details of *costs*.

I enclose details of Paris, which I *hope* will be of *interest* to you.

I look forward to *hearing* from you again.

Unit 4

1   WHAT DO YOU SAY?

1 c   2 e   3 b   4 f   5 a   6 d

2   SAYING WHAT YOU WILL DO

1 I'll take it to the cloakroom, sir.
2 I'll send some up immediately, madam.
3 I'll try his room for you, madam.
4 I'll put you through to the restaurant, sir.
5 I'll give them the message, madam.
6 I'll ask him to call you when he returns, sir.
7 I'll ring the travel agent for you, madam.
8 I'll make an appointment with the barber for you, sir.

3   GIVING ADVICE

2 It's worth going to the mountains, sir/madam. There are some beautiful views.
3 It's worth booking as early as possible, sir/madam. There's an exhibition then.
4 It's worth hiring a car, sir/madam. Public transport is not very good in the country.
5 It's worth visiting the cathedral, sir/madam. It's got some beautiful windows.
6 It's worth taking a taxi, sir/madam. They're very cheap here.
7 It's worth comparing them, sir/madam. They're very competitive.

4   ASKING WHAT THE GUEST PREFERS

1 Would you prefer/rather one room or separate rooms, sir?
2 Would you prefer to/rather pay cash or by credit card, madam?
3 Would you prefer/rather in the restaurant or outside, sir?
4 Would you prefer/rather the morning or the afternoon trip, sir?
5 Would you prefer/rather the afternoon or the evening show, madam?

5 OFFERING TO HELP
1 c 2 b 3 f 4 e 5 a 6 d

6 AT RECEPTION
Tapescript
Takako works in the Holiday Inn, Tokyo. Listen to these guests asking her questions. Then read the answers in your book. Listen to the question again and put a tick against the right answer. Here's the first guest.

GUEST: I'm booked on flight JL 511 to Heathrow tomorrow, but I need another three days here in Tokyo. Can you see if I can postpone my flight for three days?
TAKAKO: Certainly, madam. I'll see what I can do.

Number 2
GUEST: I've got an open ticket to Hong Kong. I'd like to fly there the day after tomorrow. Can you see if I can get a seat, preferably on a morning flight.
TAKAKO: I'll do my best, madam.

Number 3
GUEST: I've got to go to Osaka tomorrow. I'd like to arrive around three o'clock, so if you could get me a train ticket, first class, for sometime in the morning, that'd be fine.
TAKAKO: I'll make the booking immediately, sir.

Number 4
GUEST: I'd like to get out of the city over the weekend, and was thinking of going on some sort of trip.
TAKAKO: Did you have anything particular in mind, madam?
GUEST: Not really. A trip that includes something worth visiting. An old temple, a castle, something like that.
TAKAKO: I'll give you details of the trips we have, madam, and then you can choose the one you prefer.

Number 5
GUEST: I'm booked on flight BA 007 in two days' time. Could you just ring British Airways and confirm it for me?
TAKAKO: Of course, sir.

Key
1 b 2 c 3 c 4 a 5 c

7 TAKE THE MESSAGE
Tapescript
Listen to these guests and write down the message.

Number 1
TAKAKO: Reception, can I help you?
GUEST: Could you please ring Japan Airlines and confirm my seat on flight JL 511 tomorrow morning?
TAKAKO: Certainly, sir.

Number 2
TAKAKO: Reception, may I help you?
GUEST: Yes, I've had a look at that brochure about weekend trips you gave me earlier, and I'd like you to book two places for the weekend trip to Osaka. It's trip E6.
TAKAKO: I'll do that immediately, madam.

Number 3

TAKAKO: Reception, good morning.

GUEST: Look, I've just had a telex saying my wife has had an accident. So, can you please get me on the first flight back to London? I don't mind what class or airline, just the first available flight.

TAKAKO: I'm so sorry, sir. I'll get on to it straightaway.

Number 4

TAKAKO: Reception, good evening.

GUEST: Could you send a telex for me, please?

TAKAKO: Certainly, madam. Would you like to dictate it?

GUEST: It's to England, number 35678, answerback FFG. Attention Mr Roberts, that's R-O-B-E-R-T-S. The message reads: Flight postponed. Arriving Monday at 5.35 p.m. Regards, Park, P-A-R-K.

Key

1 confirm; JL 511.

2 2; E6.

3 b

4 NUMBER: *35678* ANSWERBACK: *FFG*
ATTENTION: Mr *Roberts*
Flight postponed. Arriving Monday at 5.35 p.m.
Regards
Park

8 SOME CONVERSATIONS

Now read the sentences in your book. Then listen to this guest. Choose the sentence that best answers what the guest says. Say that sentence onto the cassette. You will then hear the right answer. Read the sentences now.

Now here's the guest. Are you ready?

GUEST: Good afternoon.

YOU: Good afternoon, madam. How can I help you?

GUEST: My husband and I wanted to go on some sort of an excursion over the weekend. Can you suggest something?

YOU: Certainly, madam. Would you prefer a weekend excursion, or a one day trip?

GUEST: Oh, just the one day, I think.

YOU: We've got a lot of one day excursions. I'll give you the brochure, and then you can choose the one you prefer.

GUEST: Thank you. Can you make the booking for us?

YOU: Of course, madam. Tell me what you'd like, and I'll make the booking.

GUEST: Fine.

Now look at the next group of sentences. Then listen to the next guest. Again, choose the sentence that best answers what the guest says. Say that sentence onto the cassette. You will then hear the right answer. Read the sentences now.

GUEST: Can you get me a flight to Kuala Lumpur in the next couple of days, do you think?

YOU: I can certainly try, sir. Would you prefer economy, business or first class?

GUEST: Business class, please. Do you know when the flights are?

YOU: There's a morning and an evening flight, sir. Which would you prefer?

GUEST: I'd rather the morning if possible.

YOU: The morning flight. I'll ring the airline, sir, and see what I can do.

GUEST: Thank you very much. I'll be in my room, number 412.

YOU: I'll ring you as soon as I know anything, sir.

GUEST: Thank you.

9 A LETTER

MANY *THANKS* FOR YOUR LETTER *OF* 20th FEBRUARY. WE ARE VERY *PLEASED* THAT YOU HAVE ACCEPTED OUR *OFFER. SAMPLE MENUS* WILL BE SENT TO YOU IN THE NEXT FEW DAYS.

REGARDS

Dear Mr Dutton,

Further to my telex, I *enclose* sample *menus* as requested.

We would *welcome* any comments you may have on these, and would be *pleased* to make any changes you *may* want.

You will *see* that we have *included* a mixture of Japanese and Western *food*, our purpose being to *cater* for different *tastes*.

I look forward to hearing from you.

Yours sincerely,

Unit 5

I WHERE IS IT LOCATED?

1 The kitchen is situated/located in the basement.
2 The restaurant is situated/located on the mezzanine.
3 The manager's office is situated/located on the ground floor.
4 The bedrooms are situated/located on the first floor.
5 The night club is situated/located in the basement.
6 The cafeteria is situated/located on the mezzanine.
7 The cloakroom is situated/located on the ground floor.

2 GUESTS ARRIVE

2 They're/They are shown to reception.
3 They're/They are welcomed at reception.
4 They're/They are given a registration card.
5 They're/They are checked in.
6 They're/They are handed a key.
7 They're/They are taken to the lift.
8 They're/They are shown to their room.

3 GIVING ADVICE

2 I should ask at reception, sir/madam.
3 I should enquire at the lost property office, sir/madam.
4 I should ring room service, sir/madam.
5 I should call the airport, sir/madam.
6 I should go to the meeting point, sir/madam.
7 I should see the manager, sir/madam.

4 WHERE WAS IT FOUND?

1 Are these your documents, sir/madam? They were left in the bar.
2 Is this your suitcase, sir/madam? It was found in the foyer.
3 Are these your keys, sir/madam? They were handed in at reception.
4 Is this your jacket, sir/madam? It was discovered in the night club.
5 Are these your coats, sir/madam? They were put in the cloakroom.

5 MORE ADVICE

First read the sentences in your book. Then listen to these guests. Choose the sentence that best answers the guest. Say the sentence onto the cassette. You will then hear the right answer. Are you ready? Here's the first guest.

GUEST: What's the quickest way to the airport? I'm in a hurry.
YOU: I should take a taxi, sir. Shall I get one for you?

Number 2
GUEST: I've lost my purse.
YOU: I should go to the lost property office, madam. Shall I show you the way?

Number 3
GUEST: Can you help me? I need to postpone my flight by two days.
YOU: I should contact the airline, sir. Shall I call them for you?

Number 4
GUEST: I want to discuss the possibility of having a conference here.
YOU: I should speak to the manager, madam. Shall I put you through to him?

Number 5
GUEST: Where can I find some night life around here?
YOU: I should go to the old city, sir. Shall I give you a map?

6 TAKE THE MESSAGE
Tapescript
Listen to these guests and write down the message.

Number 1
RECEPTION: Holiday Inn, can I help you?
GUEST: Yes, my name's Vicini. That's V-I-C-I-N-I. I booked a table in your restaurant for ten this evening, but two of my guests can't come. Could you change the number to eight, please?
RECEPTION: Certainly, sir. I'll tell the restaurant.

Number 2
RECEPTION: Holiday Inn, good afternoon.
GUEST: I've got a reservation for six in your restaurant, and I've ordered the meal. I've just found out that one of my guests is a vegetarian. Can you arrange for him to have a vegetarian meal?
RECEPTION: I'm sure we can, madam. I'll speak to the chef about it. Could you tell me your name?
GUEST: Oh, of course, it's Lopez. L-O-P-E-Z.

Number 3
RECEPTION: Good morning, Holiday Inn.
GUEST: This is Computer International. I wanted to confirm the arrangements for our conference next month. From the third to the fifth of April. We shall need seventeen double rooms, and thirty-two single ones. So we shall be sixty-six for each meal. And we will want one large and two small conference rooms. Is that all right?
RECEPTION: That'll be fine, sir. I'll tell the manager and if there are any problems, he'll come back to you.
GUEST: Thank you.

Key
1 Vicini; eight; ten
2 Lopez; b
3 Computer International; third; fifth April; double rooms; single rooms; sixty-six; three

7 SOME CONVERSATIONS

Now read the sentences in your book. Then listen to this guest. Choose the sentence that best answers what the guest says. Say that sentence onto the cassette. You will then hear the right answer. Read the sentences now.

GUEST: Can I speak to Mr Hussein, please?
RECEPTION: I'll put you through to his room, sir.

    . . .

RECEPTION: I'm afraid there's no answer, sir. Shall I page him for you?
GUEST: No, don't worry. Tell him I'll call him at ten tomorrow morning. My name's Said.
RECEPTION: At ten tomorrow morning, sir. I'll give him the message.
GUEST: Thank you. Goodnight.
RECEPTION: Goodnight, sir.

Now look at the next group of sentences. Then listen to the next guest. Again, choose the sentence that best answers what the guest says. Say that sentence onto the cassette. You will then hear the right answers. Read the sentences now.

GUEST: Can you get me Mr Brown, please? Room 23.
RECEPTION: Certainly, madam. May I tell him who's calling?
GUEST: Miss Roberts.
RECEPTION: One moment, please. I'm putting you through now.

    . . .

BROWN: Brown.
RECEPTION: There's a Miss Roberts on the line, Mr Brown. Do you wish to take the call?
BROWN: Yes, I suppose so. Put her through.
RECEPTION: You're through now, Miss Roberts.
GUEST: Thank you. Hello, Mr Brown, I. . .

8 A LETTER

THANK YOU *FOR* YOUR LETTER. WE *REGRET* TO HEAR THAT YOU HAVE RECEIVED *COMPLAINTS* FROM YOUR DELEGATES ABOUT THE FOOD *OFFERED*. AS THE FOOD WAS AGREED BY YOURSELVES, WE DO NOT *FEEL* OBLIGED TO OFFER ANY *COMPENSATION*. LETTER FOLLOWS.

REGARDS

Dear Mr Dutton,

It was with *regret* that we *received* your letter regarding your sales conference here.

May I point out that the menus were *agreed* by yourself, well in advance of the conference, and that your *delegates* had a *choice* of food at each of the meals, *including* the final banquet.

In these *circumstances* we do not feel *obliged* to offer *compensation*, and feel sure that you will *understand* our *position*.

Yours sincerely,

Unit 6

I GIVING MESSAGES

1 She says she's arriving at 7.30.
2 She says she's expecting you in the lounge.
3 He says he's coming down to the foyer.
4 He says he's waiting in the bar.
5 He says he's leaving tomorrow.
6 She says she's sending you a fax.

2 MORE MESSAGES

2 Hello, Mr Larkins. Mrs Short says she'll be late this evening.
3 Hello, Mr Said. Mr Hussein says he'll call tomorrow afternoon.
4 Hello, Mr van der Hauwe. Miss Andreotti says she'll expect you tomorrow morning at 10.
5 Hello, Mr Singh. Mr Mohammed says he'll wait for you in the restaurant.
6 Hello, Mr Roberts. Miss Li says she'll arrive tomorrow evening.
7 Hello, Miss Porter. Mr Renard says he'll see you at the theatre.

3 SAYING YOU'RE SORRY

1 I'm terribly sorry, Mr Laporte. Miss Garcia won't be able to meet you here this evening.
2 I'm terribly sorry, Mr Schmidt. Mr Kreis won't be able to have dinner with you this evening.
3 I'm terribly sorry, Mr Pile. Miss Ogden won't be able to go to the theatre this evening.
4 I'm terribly sorry, Mr Henderson. Mrs Chan won't be able to stay an extra day.
5 I'm terribly sorry, Mr Loewenthal. Mr Isaacs won't be able to attend a meeting this afternoon.

4 WHO DO YOU SEND?

1 I'm very sorry, madam. I'll send the electrician immediately.
2 I'm very sorry, madam. I'll send the plumber immediately.
3 I'm very sorry, madam. I'll send the porter immediately.
4 I'm very sorry, madam. I'll send the manager immediately.
5 I'm very sorry, madam. I'll send the waiter immediately.

5 TAKE THE MESSAGE

Tapescript
Listen to these guests and write down the message.

Number 1
GUEST: Good evening. This is Mr Smith in room thirty-one. Please tell Mrs Gabbiadini when she comes that I won't be able to have dinner this evening. I'm ill.
RECEPTION: Certainly, sir. I'll give her the message.

Number 2
GUEST: Hello. This is Mr Leadbetter. When Mr Abrahams comes, tell him I'm waiting in the bar, would you?
RECEPTION: Of course, sir.

Number 3
GUEST: This is Miss O'Malley. Can you tell Mrs Carmichael I've been delayed at a meeting. I'll be there at around eight.
RECEPTION: I'll see Mrs Carmichael gets the message, Miss O'Malley.

Number 4
GUEST: My name's Rodrigues, room forty-seven. Please tell Mr Kleist I'll be there in half an hour.
RECEPTION: Certainly, Mr Rodrigues.

Number 5
GUEST: This is Miss Sekiguchi. Please tell Mr Macdonald I'm expecting him in the restaurant.
RECEPTION: I'll do that, Miss Sekiguchi.

Number 6
GUEST: My name's Hindmarsh. When a Mr Meier rings, can you tell him I won't be able to call him this morning. I'll ring late this afternoon.

Key

1 have dinner; evening; ill.
2 waiting; bar.
3 delayed; meeting; around eight.
4 half an hour.
5 expecting; restaurant.
6 He won't be able; late this afternoon.

6   GIVE THE MESSAGE

You have just written down some messages. Now give the right messages to the people who ask for them. Say the message onto the cassette. You will then hear the right answer. Start each message with *Hello, Mr* or *Miss* or *Mrs*, then the person's name, and then *I have a message for you. Mr*, then the name, *says*, then the message. Are you ready? Here's the first person.

CALLER: My name's Macdonald. I'm supposed to meet a Miss Sekiguchi here.
YOU: Hello, Mr Macdonald. I have a message for you. Miss Sekiguchi says she's expecting you in the restaurant.

Here's the next caller.

CALLER: It's Mrs Gabbiadini. Do you know where Mr Smith is?
YOU: Hello, Mrs Gabbiadini. I have a message for you. Mr Smith says he won't be able to have dinner this evening. He's ill.

Here's the next caller.

CALLER: My name's Abrahams. Where can I find Mr Leadbetter?
YOU: Hello, Mr Abrahams. I have a message for you. Mr Leadbetter says he's waiting in the bar.

Here's the next caller.

CALLER: My name's Meier. I was expecting a phone call from one of your guests, Mr Hindmarsh. Do you know what's happened?
YOU: Hello, Mr Meier. I have a message for you. Mr Hindmarsh says he won't be able to call you this morning. He'll ring late this afternoon.

Here's the next caller.

CALLER: My name's Mrs Carmichael. Do you know what's happened to Miss O'Malley?
YOU: Hello, Mrs Carmichael. I have a message for you. Miss O'Malley says she's been delayed at a meeting. She'll be here at around eight.

And here's the last caller.

CALLER: I was expecting to meet one of your guests here, Mr Rodrigues. My name's Kleist, by the way.
YOU: Hello, Mr Kleist. I have a message for you. Mr Rodrigues says he'll be here in half an hour.

7   SOME CONVERSATIONS

Now read the sentences in your book. Then listen to this guest. Choose the sentence that best answers what the guest says. Say that sentence onto the cassette. You will then hear the right answer. Read the sentences now.

GUEST: I'm quite sure there's something wrong with my bill, you know. It seems very high to me.
YOU: I'm terribly sorry, madam. Can you see exactly what's wrong?
GUEST: No. Not immediately. It just seems a lot.
YOU: Would you like me to check the receipts?
GUEST: Yes, please.

YOU: Here are your receipts, madam. This is your signature, isn't it? Room 409.
GUEST: That's right.
YOU: Well, I'm fairly sure the bill's correct. Would you like to check it?
GUEST: Yes, OK. Now, let me see...

Now look at the next group of sentences. Then listen to the next guest. Again, choose the sentence that best answers what the guest says. Say that sentence onto the cassette. You will then hear the right answer. Read the sentences now.

GUEST: I'm expecting to meet one of your guests here this evening, Mr Brady.
YOU: May I have your name, sir?
GUEST: Yes, it's Ollero.
YOU: One moment, sir. I'll see if Mr Brady left a message.
GUEST: Thank you.
YOU: Yes, here we are, sir. I'm afraid Mr Brady won't be able to join you for dinner, sir.
GUEST: Oh, why not?
YOU: He says his wife has had an accident. At home. He's trying to phone the hospital.
GUEST: Oh, dear. Well, there's nothing to be done about that, is there?
YOU: No, sir.
GUEST: Well, please tell him I'm extremely sorry. And give him my best wishes.
YOU: Certainly, sir.

8 A LETTER

Dear Mrs Hedges,

Thank you for *your* letter *of* 10th March. We can certainly *cater* for you and your *husband* as we have *special* bedrooms for the *disabled*. These have a *wide* door into the bathroom, which is equipped with appropriate washing and *toilet* facilities.

There are *no* steps between the street and the *entrance* to the hotel, and the *lifts* are all wide enough to take a *wheelchair*.

I have made a *provisional* booking for you and your husband, and would be *grateful* if you could *confirm* it as soon as *possible*.

Yours sincerely,

Unit 7

1 TELLING GUESTS WHAT TO DO

1 d **2** f **3** b **4** a **5** c **6** e

2 WHEN YOU CAN'T HELP

1 I'm sorry/afraid I can't help you, sir/madam. You'll have to speak/go to the travel agent.
2 I'm sorry/afraid I can't help you, sir/madam. You'll have to try another hotel.
3 I'm sorry/afraid I can't help you, sir/madam. You'll have to wait until the next one comes.
4 I'm sorry/afraid I can't help you, sir/madam. You'll have to speak to the manager.
5 I'm sorry/afraid I can't help you, sir/madam. You'll have to go to the post office.
6 I'm sorry/afraid I can't help you, sir/madam. You'll have to ring him at his office.

3 HELPING THE GUEST

1 If you follow the porter, he'll show you the way, sir.
2 If you like, I'll book you a table, sir.
3 If you give me a message, I'll see that she gets it, sir.
4 If you go out of the main entrance, you'll find a taxi rank on your left, sir.
5 If you go to the boutique, they'll be able to help you, sir.

4 PASSING MESSAGES

1 She said she would be in the bar, madam.
2 He said he would meet you at 8, madam.
3 He said he would wait in the foyer, sir.
4 She said she would arrive at 7.30, sir.
5 She said she would be in the lounge, sir.
6 He said he would come down immediately, madam.

5 TAKE THE MESSAGE

Tapescript

Listen to these guests and write down the message.

RECEPTION:	Reception, can I help you?
GUEST:	Yes, I'd like you to send a telex for me, please.
RECEPTION:	Certainly, madam.
GUEST:	It's to three, five, zero, four, two, eight. The answerback is k, l, m, and then d for Germany.
RECEPTION:	Right.
GUEST:	It's for the attention of Mr L. Davies, that's D-A-V-I-E-S. And the message reads: Mr Chan, that's C-H-A-N, is not available until next week, stop. Do you want me to stay an extra eight days, question mark. Please telex your answer by return.
RECEPTION:	Is that it, madam?
GUEST:	That's all, yes, thank you.
RECEPTION:	Holiday Inn, can I help you?
GUEST:	Yes, my name's Smith. I booked a single room for the 14th to the 18th of this month.
RECEPTION:	Yes, sir, a confirmed reservation.
GUEST:	Well for business reasons I need to change that to the 15th to the 19th. Is that all right?
RECEPTION:	I'm sure that'll be fine, sir.
RECEPTION:	Holiday Inn, can I help you?
GUEST:	Yes, I wonder, can you manage vegetarian meals?
RECEPTION:	Yes, madam, we have a special vegetarian menu at every meal.
GUEST:	Then can you reserve a double room from the 20th to the 27th. The name's Mandelbaum. That's M-A-N-D-E-L-B-A-U-M.
RECEPTION:	Certainly, madam. What time will you be arriving?
GUEST:	Around 5 o'clock in the afternoon.
RECEPTION:	We look forward to seeing you then, madam. And thank you.

Key

1 NUMBER: *350428* Answerback: *KLM D*
  ATTENTION: *Mr L. Davies*
  MESSAGE: *Mr Chan is not available until next week. Do you want me to stay an extra eight days? Please telex your answer by return.*
2 Smith; 15th; 19th; this month.
3 Mandelbaum; 20th; 27th; 5 o'clock; double room; vegetarian.

Key

1 NUMBER: *350428* Answerback: *KLM D*
  ATTENTION: *Mr L. Davies*
  MESSAGE: *Mr Chan is not available until next week. Do you want me to stay an extra eight days? Please telex your answer by return.*
2 Smith; 15th; 19th; this month.
3 Mandelbaum; 20th; 27th; 5 o'clock; double room; vegetarian.

YOU: Certainly sir. It's C-E-N-T-R-A-L, S-Q-U-A-R-E.
GUEST: And the telephone number?
YOU: Zero, two, one. Then six, three, one, two, one, double zero.
GUEST: Thank you very much.

Now here's the next guest. Listen carefully to what information the guest asks for.

GUEST: Can you tell me the telephone number of your hotel in Jeddah?
YOU: Zero two. Then double six, double one, double zero.
GUEST: And the telex number. Have you got that?
YOU: Six, double zero, seven, double five.
GUEST: Thanks. That's all.

Now here's the next guest.

GUEST: Is there a hotel in Malta?
YOU: Yes, madam, there is.
GUEST: Where is it?
YOU: It's at Tigne Street, Sliema.
GUEST: Could you spell the name of the street, please?
YOU: Certainly, madam. It's T-I-G-N-E.
GUEST: And the telex number?
YOU: One, double four, six.
GUEST: Thank you very much.

Now here's the last guest.

GUEST: Is there a Holiday Inn in Greece?
YOU: Yes, madam, there is.
GUEST: What's the address?
YOU: It's at fifty, Michalacopoulou Street, double one, five, two, eight, Athens.
GUEST: Could you spell the name of the street, please?
YOU: Certainly, madam. It's M-A-C-H-A-L-A-C-O-P-O-U-L-O-U.
GUEST: And the telephone number?
YOU: Zero, one. Then seven, two, four, eight, three, double two.
GUEST: Thanks very much.

8 A LETTER

Dear Mrs Albertini,

Thank you for your letter.

I enclose details of our hotel in Madrid. As you can see, our hotel is 13 *kilometres* from Barajas *airport* but there is *free transport* from the airport to the hotel.

We have 313 *rooms*, each of which is equipped with a *minibar*. We also have *satellite* television.

The hotel has *gift* shops, a *hairdresser*, two *restaurants* and two *bars*. We also have a *rooftop* swimming *pool*.

The hotel is three kilometres from the Museum of *Modern Art* and 3.5 kilometres from the *Prado Museum*.

If you have any further questions, please let me know.

Yours sincerely,

Unit 8

1 MAKING REQUESTS

1 e **2** b **3** f **4** c **5** a **6** d

2 WHEN DO YOU START?

2 We stop serving at 2 o'clock, sir/madam.
3 We start serving at 7 o'clock, sir/madam.
4 We stop serving at 10 o'clock, sir/madam.
5 We stop serving at 6 o'clock, sir/madam.
6 We start serving at 10 o'clock, sir/madam.
7 We start serving at 7 o'clock, sir/madam.
8 We stop serving at 10 o'clock, sir/madam.

3 WHAT DO YOU SAY?

1 I'll have/get them changed immediately, sir/madam.
2 I'll have/get them removed immediately, sir/madam.
3 I'll have/get it brought immediately, sir/madam.
4 I'll have/get it made immediately, sir/madam.
5 I'll have/get it sent immediately, sir/madam.

4 WHAT'S WRONG?

1 The mirror needs cleaning.
2 The flowers need arranging.
3 The towels need washing.
4 The ashtray needs emptying.
5 The floor needs sweeping.
6 The curtain needs replacing.

 ## 5 TAKE THE MESSAGE

Tapescript
Listen to these guests and write down the message.

RECEPTION:	Good morning, Holiday Inn.
GUEST:	Good morning. I wanted to ask about having a company dinner at your hotel. Do you cater for company dinners?
RECEPTION:	Yes, madam, we do. How many people will there be at the dinner?
GUEST:	Not very many. Twenty-five. But we want a private room. Can you manage that?
RECEPTION:	Yes, we can, madam.
GUEST:	We also want our own menu. Do you allow that? I mean, if we send you what we want, will you price it?
RECEPTION:	I must ask the manager about that, madam. Can you give me your name and phone number, and I'll get him to call you?
GUEST:	Yes, OK. The name's Prescott, P-R-E-S-C-O-double T. And the number's 456 90167.
RECEPTION:	I'll give him the message, madam, and ask him to call you as soon as he's out of his meeting.
GUEST:	Thank you.

RECEPTION: Holiday Inn, good afternoon.
GUEST: Yes, my wife is disabled, and I'm looking for a suitable hotel for a week. Do you have facilities for the disabled?
RECEPTION: Yes, sir. We have special bedrooms on the ground floor, and a special lift from the car park to the ground floor.
GUEST: Oh, good. Then can you book us from the 11th to the 18th of next month?
RECEPTION: Certainly, sir. If you'd like to give me your name, I'll reserve a room for you.
GUEST: It's Johansson. That's J-O-H-A-N-double S-O-N.
RECEPTION: Thank you, Mr Johansson.

RECEPTION: Good evening, Holiday Inn, can I help you?
GUEST: I hope so. My name's Mrs Franklin. Tell me, does your hotel have a childminding service?
RECEPTION: We don't usually, madam, no. But I'm sure we could arrange one.
GUEST: Right. Well, do you have a double room, and a room next to it with two single beds, free from the 21st to the 30th of August?
RECEPTION: I'll just check for you, madam. Would you mind holding a moment?
GUEST: Of course not.
RECEPTION: Hello? Yes, madam, we do.
GUEST: I'll take them then. Oh, and we shall need a cot in our room for the baby. Can you do that?
RECEPTION: Of course, madam. Would you like me to make the booking?
GUEST: Yes, please. The name's Franklin. F-R-A-N-K-L-I-N.
RECEPTION: Thank you. Could you confirm this in writing, please?
GUEST: Yes, I'll do that today.

Key

1 25; private room; **c**; Prescott; 456 90167.
2 disabled; 11th; 18th; Johansson.
3 childminding; double room; next to it; two; cot; 21st; 30th; August; Franklin.

 7 GIVING INFORMATION

Now here's the first guest. Use the information in your book and the conversation to help you. Say your answers onto the cassette. You will then hear the right answer. Are you ready? Here's the first guest.

GUEST: Can you tell me something about your hotel in Slough, please?
YOU: Certainly, madam. What would you like to know?
GUEST: How far is it from Heathrow Airport?
YOU: It's six and a half kilometres, madam.
GUEST: OK. Does it have an indoor swimming pool?
YOU: Yes, madam, it does.
GUEST: And can I get my hair done in the hotel?
YOU: Yes, madam, you can.
GUEST: And last question. Is there a childminding service?
YOU: No, madam, I'm afraid there isn't.

Now here's the next guest.

GUEST: I'd like some information about your hotel in Portsmouth, please.
YOU: Certainly, sir. What would you like to know?
GUEST: How far is it from Heathrow?
YOU: It's a hundred and twelve kilometres, sir.
GUEST: And do you run a bus from Heathrow to the hotel?
YOU: No, sir, we don't.
GUEST: That's a pity. Now, sporting facilities. Does it have a tennis court?
YOU: No, sir, it hasn't.

GUEST: Oh. Well, can I at least get a sauna?
YOU: Yes, sir, you can.

Now here's the last guest.

GUEST: I'd like you to tell me a bit about your hotel in Newcastle, please.
YOU: Certainly, madam. What would you like to know?
GUEST: How near to the airport is it?
YOU: It's nine kilometres, madam.
GUEST: And do you run a courtesy bus?
YOU: Yes, madam, we do.
GUEST: And can the children go swimming?
YOU: Yes, madam, they can.
GUEST: Oh, good. And is there by any chance a games room?
YOU: Yes, madam, there is.
GUEST: Oh, splendid. I'll write about a reservation.

8 A FAX

Dear Mrs Cascarino,

Thank you for your letter of . . .

Our hotel is *19* kilometres *from* Heathrow Airport. Although it does not say so in the enclosed *details*, we run a *courtesy* bus from the airport *to* the hotel.

The hotel has an *indoor* pool, and *also* a whirlpool, which I am sure your children would *enjoy*. There are many *local attractions* suitable for children, *such* as Buckingham Palace and Madame Tussaud's.

There are also *in-room* movies and we are *equipped* with satellite TV.

I enclose our *rate card* showing details of the *cost* of rooms.

I look forward to hearing from you.

Unit 9

I GIVING ADVICE

I c **2** e **3** f **4** b **5** a **6** d

2 POLITE REQUESTS

I If you'd like to hold on, I'll try and connect you.
2 If you'd like to go out of the main entrance, you'll see the taxi rank on your right.
3 If you'd like to turn right by the lifts, you'll find the bar down the corridor.
4 If you'd like to give them to me, I'll deposit them in our safe.
5 If you'd like to speak to the manager, I'll see if he's available.
6 If you'd like to follow the porter, he'll show you to your room.
7 If you'd like to give it to me, I'll get it faxed through for you.
8 If you'd like to tell me your room number, I'll see if there are any.

3 ANSWERING QUESTIONS

I It will/It'll be going in ten minutes, madam.
2 It will/It'll be leaving in quarter of an hour, madam.
3 He/She will, He/She'll be arriving at 9 o'clock, madam.
4 It will/It'll be closing in twenty minutes, madam.
5 It will/It'll be opening in half an hour, madam.
6 He/She will, He/She'll be coming at 8 o'clock, madam.

4 ASKING QUESTIONS

1 Certainly, sir. How many will you be bringing?
2 Certainly, sir. Where will you be waiting?
3 Certainly, sir. How will you be paying?
4 Certainly, sir. When will you be leaving?
5 Certainly, sir. Where will you be staying?

6 WHAT DO YOU SAY?

Listen to what these guests say and choose the sentence that best answers the guest. Say the sentence onto the cassette. You will then hear the right answer. Are you ready? Here's the first guest.

What's the best way to get to you from the airport?
If I were you, madam, I'd take our courtesy bus.

Number 2
We'd like to find out about local places of interest.
If I were you, sir, I'd go to the tourist information office.

Number 3
I need to change my flight tickets.
If I were you, madam, I'd see the travel agent.

Number 4
Is there likely to be any difficulty getting into the theatre?
If I were you, sir, I'd book tickets in advance.

Number 5
Will my valuables be safe in my room?
If I were you, madam, I'd deposit them in our safe.

Number 6
Is your hairdresser busy as a rule?
If I were you, madam, I'd make an appointment.

7 GIVING INFORMATION

Now answer these guests' questions about the hotel. Say your answers onto the cassette. You will then hear the right answer. Here's number 1.

Do you have a swimming pool?
Yes, sir, we do.

Number 2
Do you have a tennis court?
No, madam, I'm afraid we don't.

Number 3
Do you run a courtesy bus from the airport?
Yes, madam, we do.

Number 4
Do you have facilities to keep fit?
Yes, sir, we do.

Number 5
Do you have a playground for children?
No, sir, I'm afraid we don't.

Number 6
Do you have a car park?
Yes, madam, we do.

Now look at the information about the Holiday Inn in Casablanca, Morocco. Again answer the guests' questions. Say your answer onto the cassette. Here's the first guest.

Are there car rental facilities?
Yes, sir, there are.

Number 2
Is there a tennis court?
No, madam, I'm afraid there isn't.

Number 3
Is there a swimming pool?
Yes, sir, there is.

Number 4
Is there a courtesy bus from the airport?
No, sir, I'm afraid there isn't.

Number 5
Is there dancing?
Yes, madam, there is.

Number 6
Are there any facilities for conferences?
Yes, sir, there are.

8 A LETTER

Thank you for your letter of . . .

We can certainly cater for 100 delegates as we have 364 bedrooms. Our meeting rooms can hold up to 600.

As regards sporting facilities, we have an indoor pool and fitness equipment, but unfortunately no tennis courts.

I enclose full details of the services we can offer and also of our rates.

Unit 10

I SOME CONVERSATIONS

Listen to what these guests say and choose the sentence that best answers the guest. Say the sentence onto the cassette. You will then hear the right answer.

GUEST: Good evening.
YOU: Good evening, madam. May I help you?
GUEST: Yes, my name's Johansson. Mrs Johansson. I booked a single room for three nights.
YOU: One moment, madam. I'll check.
GUEST: Thank you.
YOU: Yes, that's right. A single room with shower for three nights.
GUEST: Good.
YOU: Would you like to fill in the registration card, please?
GUEST: Right. Have you got a pen?
YOU: There's one on the desk there, madam.
GUEST: Oh, sorry. I didn't see it.

Here's the second conversation.

YOU: Holiday Inn, can I help you?
GUEST: Yes, have you got a double room free for tonight?
YOU: I'm very sorry, sir, I'm afraid we're full tonight.
GUEST: Oh dear. Can you suggest somewhere else?
YOU: If I were you, sir, I'd try the Europa. Would you like their telephone number?
GUEST: Yes, please.
YOU: It's 472 3981.
GUEST: Thank you very much.
YOU: Not at all, sir. I'm sorry we can't help you.

Here's the next conversation.

YOU: Holiday Inn, good evening.
GUEST: Yes, I'm thinking of bringing my family to your hotel for our summer holiday. But first, can you tell me about your facilities.
YOU: Certainly, sir. What would you like to know?
GUEST: Well, we have two children. Do you have any facilities for them?
YOU: Yes, sir, we do. We've got a swimming pool and a playground. We also have a games room.
GUEST: And what about TV?
YOU: There's TV in every room, sir. We've got satellite TV as well.
GUEST: Fine. Now, can I hire a car when we get there?
YOU: Yes, sir, you can.
GUEST: OK. Now, we'll be coming by air. How do we get from the airport to the hotel?
YOU: We run a courtesy bus every half hour, sir.
GUEST: Right. Can I make a booking by telephone?
YOU: Certainly, sir. How many rooms would you like? And when will you be arriving?
GUEST: One double room and two single rooms. From the first of August for two weeks.
YOU: I'll reserve those rooms for you, sir. Can you tell me your name?
GUEST: It's Smith.
YOU: Mr Smith. Would you mind confirming this, sir?
GUEST: I'll do that.
YOU: Thank you very much, sir. Goodbye.
GUEST: Goodbye.

2 WHAT DO YOU SAY?

1 d 2 f 3 a 4 e 5 c 6 b

3 A TELEX

MANY *THANKS* FOR YOUR *ENQUIRY* ABOUT TWO DOUBLE ROOMS *FOR* THE NIGHTS OF 20TH *TO* 30TH AUGUST. WE *CONFIRM* YOUR *RESERVATION*, LETTER *FOLLOWS.*

REGARDS

T. SEKIGUCHI

4 A LETTER

Dear Mr Robinson,

Thank you *for* your enquiry *about* the *facilities* our hotel can offer for family *holidays.*

I *enclose* our *brochure,* from which you will *see* that we have a games room, a children's *playground* and *also* a swimming pool.

We *run* a *courtesy* bus to and from the airport. The *journey* takes about 20 minutes.

I *suggest* you make an *early* reservation, as we are often very *full* during the months of July and August.

I *look forward* to hearing from you.

Yours *sincerely*,

H. J. Kleist (Mrs)

 5 TAKE THE MESSAGE

Tapescript

Listen to these guests and write down the message. Here's the first guest.

GUEST: Good evening, my name's Larsson. L-A-R-S-S-O-N.
RECEPTION: Yes, madam, how can I help you?
GUEST: I've been delayed, so won't arrive on the 12th of January. I'll be arriving on the 13th, and would like to stay until the 18th, not the 17th. Will that be all right?
RECEPTION: Certainly, madam.

Here's the next guest.

GUEST: Good morning. It's room four double five. I'm expecting a Mr Hussein for lunch. Can you tell him I'll wait for him in the restaurant. He should arrive at about 12.30.
RECEPTION: Could you spell the gentleman's name, please?
GUEST: H-U-double S-E-I-N.
RECEPTION: Thank you, sir. I'll give him the message.

Here's the next guest.

GUEST: Please tell Mrs Lomax, L-O-M-A-X, in room two hundred that I've been delayed in a meeting. I'll be about 45 minutes late. My name's Smith.
RECEPTION: Certainly, sir. I'll give her the message.

Here's the next guest.

GUEST: My husband's disabled. So can you make sure we get a room on the ground floor, please?
RECEPTION: Certainly, madam.

Here's the next guest.

GUEST: Good evening. I am thinking of holding a company dinner at your hotel. On the 10th of December. Can you please let me have two or three suggested menus?
RECEPTION: Certainly, sir. How many guests will there be?
GUEST: Fifty. And we'd want a private bar as well. Can that be arranged?
RECEPTION: I'm sure it can, sir. Can you give me . . .

Here's the next guest.

GUEST: I'd like to reserve a table for six for dinner tonight, please. Eight o'clock. And my name's Yamamoto. That's Y-A-M-A-M-O-T-O.
RECEPTION: Certainly, sir. I'll tell the restaurant.
GUEST: I'd like a table on the terrace, please, outside.
RECEPTION: I'll see if that can be arranged, sir.

Here's the next guest.

GUEST: Good morning. I'd like to make a reservation, please.
RECEPTION: Certainly, madam.
GUEST: The name's Andreotti. A-N-D-R-E-O-double T-I. A double room for myself and my husband, and two single rooms for the children. We'll be arriving on the 10th and staying until the 12th.
RECEPTION: That's fine, madam.

GUEST: And I'll need a cot in our room for the baby.
RECEPTION: I'll arrange that for you, madam.
GUEST: Thank you.

Here's the next guest.

GUEST: Could you send this telex, please?
RECEPTION: Certainly, madam. Would you like to dictate it?
GUEST: It's to 56386 in Germany. The answerback is LG. Attention Mr Holz. H-O-L-Z.
RECEPTION: Right.
GUEST: And the message reads:
Flight cancelled. Cannot arrive tomorrow. Will arrive on 17th by flight BA 243 at 14.30. Will come straight to your office. Apologies. Regards. Jones. J-O-N-E-S.
RECEPTION: I'll send it immediately, madam.

Key
1 Larsson; 13th; 18th.
2 455; Mr Hussein; restaurant; 12.30.
3 Smith; Lomax; 45; meeting.
4 ground floor; disabled.
5 dinner; 10th December; 50; menus; private bar.
6 Yamamoto; 6; 8; on the terrace/outside.
7 Andreotti; double; single rooms; cot; double room; 10th; 12th.
8 56386; Germany; LG; Mr Holz; Flight cancelled. Cannot arrive tomorrow. Will arrive on 17th by flight BA 243 at 14.30. Will come straight to your office. Apologies. Regards. Jones.

6 A FAX

Dear Miss Dupont,

Thank you for *your* letter of 15th April.

I *regret* we cannot *cater* for your annual sales *conference*, as we do not have the two hundred *bedrooms* you require.

However, the Holiday Inn hotel *in* Frankfurt would *be able to* meet your *requirements*, and I have *sent* your letter on to the Manager.

I am sure you *will be hearing* from him soon.

Yours truly,

M. Schneider

7 A LETTER

Dear Mr Renard,

To confirm our telex of 15th June, we can certainly *cater* for your conference *in* January next year. I enclose full *details* of our *facilities*, which I hope you will find *satisfactory*.

I *particularly* draw your attention to our *sporting* facilities, which I am sure many of your *delegates* will find useful and *relaxing*.

As *requested*, I enclose *sample* menus for your consideration. These can, of course, be *changed* should you wish.

Yours sincerely,

N. Flamand

8 GIVING INFORMATION

Some guests are asking questions about these hotels. Use the information and answer their questions. The first guest is asking about the hotel in Kuala Lumpur.

GUEST: Can you tell me, your hotel in Kuala Lumpur. Is there a swimming pool?
YOU: Yes, there is.
GUEST: And can I rent a car from the hotel?
YOU: No, I'm afraid you can't.
GUEST: And are there any sporting facilities?
YOU: Yes, there are.
GUEST: And are there any business facilities?
YOU: Yes, there are.

Now look at the information about the Singapore-Royal.
Answer this guest's questions.

GUEST: Have you got a tennis court?
YOU: No, I'm afraid we haven't.
GUEST: Are there any business facilities?
YOU: No, I'm afraid there aren't.
GUEST: Can I rent a car when I get there?
YOU: Yes, you can.
GUEST: What about fitness equipment. Have you got that?
YOU: Yes, we have.

Now look at the information about the hotel in Pakistan.
Answer this guest's questions.

GUEST: Tell me, is there a bar?
YOU: No, I'm afraid there isn't.
GUEST: Are there minibars in the rooms?
YOU: Yes, there are.
GUEST: Do you cater for conferences?
YOU: Yes, we do.
GUEST: Do you have an outdoor pool?
YOU: No, I'm afraid we don't.

GRAMMAR SUMMARY

Use this Grammar Summary to help you understand the exercises.

Unit 1

1 WHAT DO THEY DO?

The verb *to be*.
I am OR *I'm; you are* OR *you're; he/she/it is* OR *he's, she's, it's; we are* OR *we're; they are* OR *they're.*

The Present Simple
I work; you work; he/she/it works; we work; they work.
Remember to add *-s* or *-es* after he, she or it.
Use the Present Simple to talk about habits, for example:
I work in a hotel.
My friend goes to work by bus.

To ask a question, use *Do* (with I, you, we, they) or *Does* (with he, she, it), like this:
Do you speak English?
Does she work in the restaurant?

To make the negative, use *do not/don't* (with I, you, we, they) or *does not/doesn't* (with he, she, it), like this:
I do not/don't work in the bar.
She does not/doesn't speak English.

2 THE GRAND HOTEL

The verb *have got*.
I have got OR *I've got; you have got* OR *you've got; he, she, it has got* OR *he's, she's, it's got; we have got* OR *we've got; they have got* OR *they've got.*

3 WHAT DO YOU SAY?

You use *may* or *can* to ask the guest's permission for you to do something, like this:
Can (OR *May*) *I help you, sir?*

4 TELL THE GUEST THE WAY

Use a verb by itself when you are telling a guest what to do, like this:
Turn right, madam.
Ask at the front office, sir.

Unit 2

1 WHAT DO YOU SAY?

Use *Would you like to . . .?* when you want to invite the guest to do something, like this:
Would you like to sit down, madam?
Would you like to have a drink, sir?

2 ASKING QUESTIONS

These words help you ask questions: *when, where, what, how, who.*
Remember to use the question form after these words, like this:
I work in the bar.
*What time **do you begin** work?*

3 ANSWERING QUESTIONS

Look at Unit 1, Exercise 1: The Present Simple.

4 ANSWER THE GUESTS' QUESTIONS

The Past Simple

Use the Past Simple when you are talking about events that happened in the past.
To make the Past Simple, you usually add -d or -ed to the verb, like this:
I work (Present Simple) → *I work**ed*** (Past Simple).
Some verbs do not do this. They change, for example:
I go (Present Simple) → *I went* (Past Simple).

To ask a question about the past, use *Did*, like this:
Did you work last night?
Notice that when you use *Did* you do not add -d or -ed.
You do not use the past form of the verb.
Did you go to the cinema yesterday? (NOT Did you went . . .)

To make the negative, use *did not* or *didn't*, like this:
I did not/didn't work yesterday.
Again, do not use the past form of the verb.

6 SAYING *NO* POLITELY

Look at Exercise 4 above.

Unit 3

1 ASKING QUESTIONS

The Present Perfect
Use the Present Perfect when you are talking about events in the past which have a strong connection with the present.
I have lost my pen. (so now I can't write)
You also use the Present Perfect for events that started in the past but which are still continuing, like this:
I have worked in this hotel for five months. (and I am still working here)
To make the Present Perfect, use *have* or *has* and the participle. Most verbs have the same participle as their Past Simple, -d or -ed, for example,

PRESENT SIMPLE	PAST SIMPLE	PARTICIPLE	PRESENT PERFECT
I work	I worked	worked	I have worked
			He has worked

Some verbs change, like this:

PRESENT SIMPLE	PAST SIMPLE	PARTICIPLE	PRESENT PERFECT
I go	I went	gone	I have gone
			He has gone

To ask a question, change the order of *I have, The waiter has*, like this:
I have worked . . .
Have I worked . . .?
The waiter has worked . . .
Has the waiter worked . . .?

To make the negative, add *not*, like this:
I have not (or haven't) worked . . .
She has not (or hasn't) worked . . .

2 SOME MORE QUESTIONS

Look at Exercise I above.

3 WHAT'S THE BEST ANSWER?

Look at Exercise I above.

4 SOME SHORT ANSWERS

We usually answer questions using a short form. There are two ways to answer a question.
In a full sentence, like this:
Have you seen my briefcase?
Yes, I have seen your briefcase.
OR
No, I haven't seen your briefcase.
But we usually use a short answer, like this:
Have you seen my briefcase?
Yes, I have.
No, I haven't.
You usually repeat the verb the guest uses in his question, like this:
Can I see the manager?
Yes, you can.

5 HE MAY HAVE GONE TO THE BAR

You use *may* and *could* to talk about events that are possible, like this:
He may be in the bar. (It's possible he is in the bar, but I don't know.)
She could be in her room. (It's possible she is in her room, but I don't know.)
When you talk about a possible event in the past, you use *may/could*, then *have*, then the participle (*worked*, *gone* and so on), like this:
He may have left the hotel. (It's possible that he has left the hotel.)

6 TALKING TO GUESTS

You usually use words like this starting with *any-* and *no-* in negative sentences and in questions. You usually use words starting with *some-* in affirmative (yes) sentences.

Unit 4

I WHAT DO YOU SAY?

You use *will* or *'ll* when you are promising to do something for a guest, like this:
I'll (OR *I will*) *get the manager, madam.*

2 SAYING WHAT YOU WILL DO

Look at Exercise I above.

3 GIVING ADVICE

You can use *worth* when you are giving a guest advice about what to do or see. Notice that after the word *worth* you must add *-ing* to the verb, like this:
It's worth visiting the old town.

4 ASKING WHAT THE GUEST PREFERS

You can use *prefer* or *rather* when you are giving the guest a choice.

5 OFFERING TO HELP

You can use *shall* when you are offering to help a guest.

Unit 5

1 WHERE IS IT LOCATED?

The Present Simple Passive
You usually use the passive when what is done is more important than who does it, for example,
The room is booked.
Here what has happened to the place is more important than who did it.
You make the Present Simple Passive by using *I am, you are, he/she/it is, we are, they are*
and then the participle, like this:
It is situated in the foyer.
The beds are made.

2 GUESTS ARRIVE

See Exercise 1 above.

3 GIVING ADVICE

You can also use *should* when you are giving a guest advice, like this:
I should take a taxi, madam.

4 WHERE WAS IT FOUND?

The Past Simple Passive
You make the Past Simple Passive by using *was/were* and the participle, like this:
The bill was paid by credit card.
They were found in the dining room.

Unit 6

1 GIVING MESSAGES

When you give a message, you are often reporting what someone else has said. You can
do this by using *he/she says . . .*

2 MORE MESSAGES

See Exercise 1 above.

3 SAYING YOU'RE SORRY

You use *will/won't be able to* as the future of *can*.
You can swim now. The pool is open.
You won't be able to swim tomorrow. The pool will be closed.

4 WHO DO YOU SEND?

See Unit 4, Exercise 1.

Unit 7

1 TELLING GUESTS WHAT TO DO

You use *must* or *must not/mustn't* when you are giving a guest an order, like this:
You must leave at once, sir.

2 WHEN YOU CAN'T HELP

You use *will/'ll have to* when you are saying what the guest must do in the future. You can
also use *must*, like this:

You must leave tomorrow, sir.
You'll have to leave tomorrow, madam.

3 HELPING THE GUEST

We call this Conditional 1. You can use Conditional 1 when you are offering to help a guest.
Notice that a Conditional 1 sentence has two parts. One starts with the word *if*.
You usually use the Present Simple in the *if*-part of the sentence, and *will/'ll* in the other part, like this:
*If you **like**, I **will/'ll** get the manager.*

4 PASSING MESSAGES

This is another way of reporting (Unit 6, Exercise 1).
Notice that when you use *he/she says* (in the Present Simple) you do not change the tense of the verb, like this:

GUEST: *Tell Mr Smith **I am** (Present Simple) in the bar.*

When you give the message, you say:
YOU: *Mr Smith says **he is** (Present Simple) in the bar.*

When you use *he/she said* (Past Simple) you must change the tense. There are rules for this.
will becomes *would*, like this:

GUEST: *Tell Mr Smith I**'ll** telephone him.*

When you give the message you say:
YOU: *Mr Smith said he **would** telephone you.*

Unit 8

1 MAKING REQUESTS

You can use *Would you mind . . .?* as a polite way of asking a guest to do something. Notice that after *Would you mind . . .?* you must add *-ing* to the verb, like this:
Would you mind waiting a moment, madam?

2 WHEN DO YOU START?

After most English verbs you use *to*, for example:
*I want **to book** a table, please.*
After some English verbs you can use either *to* or you can add *-ing* to the verb, for example:
*We start **to serve** dinner at 8 o'clock.*
*We start **serving** dinner at 8 o'clock.*
After some verbs you must add *-ing*, for example,
*I enjoyed **staying** at your hotel.*
Verbs which must have *-ing* are:

> finish, prevent, risk, admit, delay, postpone, enjoy, forgive, pardon, excuse, suggest,
> keep (= continue), stop (= cease), understand, miss, involve, save.

There are others, but you will probably not need them.

3 WHAT DO YOU SAY?

You can use *will have* or *will get* and then the participle when you are promising to help a guest, but will not do it yourself, for example,
I'll get your room cleaned, madam. (Here, you won't clean the room yourself, but will make sure someone cleans it.)

4 WHAT'S WRONG?

Need is one of the verbs you can follow with *to* or you can add *-ing*. In Exercise 4 in Unit 8 add *-ing*.

Unit 9

I GIVING ADVICE

You can also use *If I were you* when you give a guest advice. Notice that in the second part of the sentence you use *would/'d* not *will* as in Conditional I, like this:
If I were you, I would/'d take a taxi, madam.

2 POLITE REQUESTS

This is a way to ask your guests questions politely. You use *If you'd like to . . .* Notice that in the second part of your request you use *will*, like this:
If you'd like to tell me your name, I'll check your reservation.

3 ANSWERING QUESTIONS

This is the Future Continuous.
You use the Future Continuous for events that are about to happen in the near future, like this:
It'll be closing in five minutes, madam.
You make the Future Continuous with *will*, then *be* and then the verb with *-ing*.

4 ASKING QUESTIONS

You can also use the Future Continuous for future events that are planned, like this:
When will you be arriving, sir?
I'll be arriving at 8 o'clock.

Unit 10

There is no new grammar in Unit 10.